THIRD EDITION

Enforcing Ethics

A Scenario-Based Workbook
for Police and Corrections Recruits and Officers

DEBBIE J. GOODMAN, M.S.

Miami Dade College
School of Justice
Miami, Florida

PEARSON

Prentice
Hall

Upper Saddle River, New Jersey 07458

Library of Congress Cataloging-in-Publication Data
Goodman, Debbie J.
   Enforcing ethics: a scenario-based workbook for police and
corrections recruits and officers/Debbie J. Goodman.—3rd ed.
      p. cm.
Includes bibliographical references.
   ISBN-13: 978-0-13-225649 0
   ISBN-10: 0-13-225649-5
   1. Police ethics—Problems, exercises, etc. 2. Correctional
personnel—Professional ethics—Problems, exercises, etc. I. Title.
   HV7924 .G66 2008
   174'.93632—dc21

Editor-in-Chief: Vernon R. Anthony
Senior Editor: Tim Peyton
Associate Editor: Sarah Holle
Marketing Manager: Adam Kloza
Managing Editor: Mary Carnis
Production Liaison: Ann Pulido
Production Editor: Jessica Balch, Pine Tree
   Composition
Manufacturing Manager: Ilene Sanford

Manufacturing Buyer: Cathleen Petersen
Senior Design Coordinator: Miguel Ortiz
Cover Designer: Jill Little, iDesign
Cover Image: Florian Frank, Jupiter Images/
   Brand X Pictures
Composition: Laserwords Private Limited,
   Chennai, India
Cover Printer: Phoenix Color
Printing and Binding: Bind-Rite Graphics

Pearson Education LTD.
Pearson Education Australia PTY, Limited
Pearson Education Singapore, Pte. Ltd.
Pearson Education North Asia Ltd.
Pearson Education Canada, Ltd.
Pearson Education de Mexico, S.A. de C.V.
Pearson Education—Japan
Pearson Education Malaysia, Pte. Ltd.
Pearson Education Upper Saddle River, New Jersey

10 9 8 7 6
ISBN-13: 978-0-13-225649-0
ISBN-10: 0-13-225649-5

For Glenn,

my love, my life

For Connor and Carson,

my sons, my suns

Contents

Preface

Some homes look like castles on the outside and cottages on the inside. They appear to be one way but are not, in reality, what they seem to be.

The criminal justice profession is like a castle: prestigious, prominent, and deserving of respect. It is critical that the inhabitants of the castle, *all* officers who have sworn to uphold and enforce the law, conduct themselves in accordance with appropriate standards of behavior.

The profession must be what it is designed to be: equitable, effective, and ethical. Anything less is unacceptable.

The third edition of *Enforcing Ethics* has a fundamental purpose: to encourage you, the skilled police or corrections recruit or officer, to think critically and carefully about your behavior, your decisions, and your values.

The new edition of *Enforcing Ethics* includes more realistic, timely scenarios, for you to explore with your colleagues and trainers. The scenarios present true-to-life matters, from the basic to the complex, ethical dilemmas that you may be faced with during the scope of your career. Also, additional information is included in Chapter 1 regarding forms of police deviance you will hopefully avoid during your professional career.

Enforcing Ethics will introduce you to *ethical encounters;* also, you will analyze *points to ponder:* questions to discuss among your colleagues.

Enforcing Ethics will likely lead to opposing points of view, heated discussions, and intense debates. That's fine. In whatever environment you choose to cover the material, keep one goal in mind: to answer truthfully and openly.

Enjoy *Enforcing Ethics,* and thank you for serving our communities with pride, honesty, and integrity.

Acknowledgments

To my wonderful family: I love you, Mom, Dad, Corinne, Sam, Sol, Alan, Andy, Bruce, Marisela, Jane, Marion, Mark, Harris, Brooke, Stephen, Christopher, Eddie, Lisa, and Amy.

To the students, faculty, staff, and administrators of Miami Dade College and the School of Justice: Thank you for your support, Dr. Eduardo Padron, Dr. Jeffrey Lukenbill, Dr. Jose Vicente, Ron Grimming, Dr. Donna Jennings, Tom Hood, Anna Leggett, Ed Hargis, Sam Latimore, Fred Hutchings, Scott Davis, Mike Grimes, Clyde Pfleegor, Miriam Lorenzo, Clark Zen, Jean Doubles, and many others.

To the criminal justice professionals who reviewed the workbook: Thank you for your expertise: Chief Curtis Ivy, Chief William Berger, Chief Patrick Kelly, Chief Tom Hood, Captain Miguel Exposito, Superintendent Marta Villacorta, Captain Rebecca Tharpe, Officer Bernard Bullock, Vincent J. Petrarca, Brad Farnsworth, Michael T. Charles, and Dan Durkee. I would also like to thank Luis Hernandez, Hillsborough Community College, Wesley Chapel, FL; Allan Jiao, Rowan University, Glassboro, NJ; and Len Supenski, Harrisburg Community College, Gettysburg, for reviewing this edition of *Enforcing Ethics.*

To Robin Baliszewski, Tim Peyton, Sarah Holle, Adam Kloza, and the dedicated staff at Prentice Hall, as well as Jessica Balch and the staff at Pine Tree Composition: Thank you for your efforts on behalf of the workbook.

To Mary Greene: Thank you for your typing and manuscript assistance.

To the men and women of law enforcement and corrections: Thank you for your exceptional service to our communities.

About the Author

Debbie J. Goodman, M.S., is the Chairperson of the School of Justice at Miami Dade College in Miami, Florida. She is the published author of *Report It in Writing, Florida Crime and Justice, The Search and Seizure Handbook, The Criminal Justice Reality Reading Series,* and *Work in Criminal Justice.* She was honored in 2002 and 2005 by *Who's Who Among America's College Instructors* as one of the nation's most talented college instructors. She is an adjunct professor for Florida International University's School of Policy Management. Ms. Goodman resides in southern Florida with her husband and sons.

1

Exploring Ethics

You come home from an emotionally and physically exhausting shift. Today you encountered a suicidal juvenile who listened to your words of encouragement and allowed you to help her. You also apprehended a subject who has been involved in a string of unsolved burglaries. It's fair to say that you put in a "hard day's work." Nice job, Officer! While relaxing at home, you turn on the TV set and "channel surf" through the programs. You hear a news reporter announce, "Late this afternoon, officers went to the apartment of Officer Ray Hammond and arrested their fellow colleague for grand theft. Internal Affairs (IA) investigators claim they have a videotape of Hammond stealing stereo equipment, computers, and cellular phones from local businesses. Officials tell us an in-depth investigation is underway."

What did you just hear? An officer who has *sworn* to protect the citizens and enforce the laws has been arrested for *intentionally* violating the law to achieve personal gain? Disgusted by this information, you turn off the television and skim the newspaper. After reading the national news, you turn to the local section of the paper. Your attention is drawn to the headline: *Corrections Officers from County Jail Allow Drugs to Enter Facility.* You sit back in your chair, close your eyes, and wonder, "What's going on here?"

What's going on, Officer, is an eye-opening reality check. Unethical behavior has become increasingly prevalent in what many are calling the "morally deficient society" in which we live. When citizens read or hear about children bringing guns to school, elderly women being brutally raped, and marriages turning bitter and ending in bloodshed, a universal cry for help can be heard in nearly every large city within the United States. To whom do we turn for help? Officers, of course!

Each and every time an officer in any city, county, or state participates in unethical conduct, the entire law enforcement and corrections profession is adversely affected. Clearly, most officers are responsible, dedicated, and ethical. It's unfortunate that *you*, the heroes in the criminal justice field, are not given nearly enough positive attention and recognition, which you rightfully deserve. Officers deserve respect and support; at the same time, citizens deserve peace of mind. One way to give citizens this is to conduct yourself as a *professional* each day for the rest of your career. Whether it's fair or not, whether it's valid or not, people tend to group and judge and categorize others. Often, officers are not viewed individually but collectively. Therefore, if a citizen has had one negative encounter with one officer, chances are the citizen will regard *all* officers in a less-than-favorable manner. Can you afford that? No! So what's an officer to do? Although it is unrealistic to believe that every person walking the planet will regard every officer respectfully, it may be more realistic to believe that every officer walking the "beat" or the "cat walk" can conduct himself or herself in a respectful, professional, and ethical manner. Your conduct leads to how others regard you, treat you, and react to your role. Your role is unlike any other; therefore, your behavior must be sterling or the badge, as well as the profession, may become tarnished. Let's begin our discussion of the study of ethics.

A Higher Standard

The vast majority of police officers are ethical. Unfortunately, as in any profession, there is a certain percentage of officers who act unethically. Some of these individuals were already "bad" when they first became officers, while others became "bad" through years of exposure to the temptations of their job. Some police officers become lawbreakers themselves in their quest for more power, more money, or both.

Since a certain percentage of society, and the professions that represent society, will act in an unethical manner, what's the point of even teaching ethics? If our police officers are a representation of society, isn't it unavoidable that some of them will "go bad," so to speak? My answer to that is a resounding *NO!* Although it is perceived that police are and should be representative of society as a whole, they are and should be representative of ethical society, not society as a whole.

Police should be held to a higher standard. I firmly believe that! What do you think about officers being held to a higher standard?

_____

_____

_____

Serpico: Hero or Rat?

Frank Serpico was a New York police officer for 15 years. During that time, Serpico repeatedly turned down payoffs and turned in corrupt fellow officers. He was shot during a drug raid that he claims was a setup.

Today, Serpico still urges police departments to pierce the "blue wall of silence." "We must create an atmosphere where the crooked cop fears the honest cop, and not the other way around."

He believes, unfortunately, that not much has changed in his department. Take the 1997 incident of Haitian immigrant Abner Louima, who accused four New York City police officers of beating and sodomizing him inside a police station. The cops were eventually found guilty—proof, according to Serpico, that not much has changed. Serpico believes that the cop culture is infected with brutality, corruption, and racism and is immune to quick-fix solutions.

What is your opinion?

_____

_____

_____

_____

_____

_____

_____

_____

According to Serpico, the solution to police corruption is the following: (1) stricter supervision and accountability, (2) better pay for street cops, (3) mandatory and regular psychological evaluations, and (4) support (not lip service) for officers who report wrongdoing.

Let's discuss each of his points.

Stricter Supervision and Accountability

What are your people doing, Managers? Good leadership, according to most law enforcement managers, involves the following:

- Managing personnel in the field
- Supervising patrol activities

- Conducting inspections
- Maintaining discipline
- Enforcing rules and regulations
- Conducting roll call
- Managing field operations

Better Pay for Street Cops

Increasing police officers' pay is a straightforward and obvious way to decrease unethical behavior both on and off the job by decreasing their need for more money. In addition, increasing pay would increase the number and quality of applicants interested in becoming police officers. This would allow police departments to choose new recruits from a higher caliber of individuals.

Mandatory and Regular Psychological Evaluations

In order to nip a problem in the bud before it causes problems, psychological evaluations of officers on a regular basis are an important tool. In order for this to be effective, these evaluations must be done in the strictest of confidence, so that officers will not be worried about the results and who might find out. Employing psychological professionals not located within the department itself may be a way for officers to feel more comfortable with the process.

Support (Not Lip Service) for Officers Who Report Wrongdoing

Supervisors have to have complete control and understanding of what's going on with their officers. The officers must have respect for their supervisors in order for this relationship to be effective. Promoting an officer to supervisor prematurely (before the officer has paid his or her dues on the job, so to speak) could be a problem. If an officer screws up on the job, he or she will definitely be held accountable. But it's the supervisor who is ultimately responsible.

Leadership among law enforcement managers involves managing line personnel in the field. It takes courage and a solid conviction of what's right and moral to turn in one of your own. Therefore, supervisors need to ensure that those officers who come forward with information on corruption, brutality, or other misconduct are protected. Unfortunately, the "good guy" may be perceived as the "bad guy," depending on how the investigations are handled from the beginning. The Whistle Blowers Act was implemented to afford officers the necessary protection needed in these circumstances. Always remember the strength and courage it takes to do the right thing versus the weakness and cowardice to do what's wrong. Supervisors play a crucial role in how ethically subordinates conduct themselves. What do you think about Serpico's four recommendations for reducing police corruption?

1. Stricter supervision and accountability

    _____

    _____

    _____

    _____

    _____

2. Better pay for street cops

    _____

    _____

    _____

    _____

    _____

3. Mandatory and regular psychological evaluations

    _____

    _____

    _____

    _____

    _____

4. Support (not lip service) for officers who report wrongdoing

    _____

    _____

    _____

    _____

    _____

So, then, what does it mean to hold officers to a higher standard? It means that their behavior, conduct, speech, attitude, and demeanor must be better than that of the rest of the world.

Yeah . . . But . . .

Ethics, by definition, is the study of morals—good vs. bad, right vs. wrong. Plain and simple. We're not going to talk about Plato or Aristotle; for our purposes, getting into the history of philosophers, theorists, and ethicists and their views, their perceptions, and their arguments is not necessary at this time.

What is necessary is that we in the criminal justice profession recognize right from wrong, practice it, believe it, uphold it, and enforce it.

"Yeah, you're right . . . but . . ." But what?! I hear this all the time from students, colleagues, officers, police chiefs, prosecutors, and trainees.

No excuses. No shortcuts. No turning the other cheek. Just do it. Do what is right, moral, just, legal, and appropriate. Those who like to give the "Yeah . . . but . . ." argument are telling us that they lack the power, control, and discipline upon which the foundation of this profession is based.

Every day officers must exercise power, control, and discipline, on and off duty. How difficult is it to be courteous, pay for your own stuff, tell the truth, do the best job you are capable of doing, and enforce and uphold the laws of the state in which you live? What's the problem? Let's stick with "Yeah!" instead of "Yeah . . . but . . . ."

Ethics Is a Choice

OK, so now you're coming around a bit. I don't expect you to see it my way, not yet. Not entirely anyway. Let me try to further convince you. You realize that as an officer you're in a fishbowl for all to see. People are watching. We love to watch others. Voyeurism? Could be. Whatever you call it, its reality. So let's be real. If people are watching what you say and do, then how do you want to be perceived?

_____

_____

_____

_____

How you want and choose to be perceived will ultimately determine what you become. Ethics is a choice; it's not a fancy concept. It's a choice, so if you choose to be ethical, A to Z, soup to nuts, without the "Yeah . . . buts," then let's talk.

Making an Ethical Decision

Making an ethical decision, whether it is a personal or professional one, is based on Goodman's ABCD formula:

Actions
Beliefs
Conduct
Discipline

Actions

The way you act, the actions you take day to day, will determine results. Exercise is a good example. Eat well, exercise, don't smoke, don't drink (or if you do, only in moderation), and manage stress, and you should be relatively healthy, according to most doctors. Be intelligent, be hard-working, don't lie, don't cheat, don't steal, and do your best, and you should stay clear of any Internal Affairs (IA) investigations.

Beliefs

Believe in yourself, your department, your profession, your family, your religion, your friends. Believe in the laws of the land, the policies and procedures of your department, the good of the cause. Believe that ours is a noble profession and stand firm on those beliefs. Believe that you can make a positive difference each and every day. Believe that good guys (and gals) prevail and that the bad ones need to be punished.

Conduct

Conduct yourself as if everyone were watching: Mom, Dad, Wife, Uncle, Chief, Son, God. How do you want them to see you? Let them see you as an honorable, trustworthy, dedicated officer. Let them be proud of you and your actions, not shamed and embarrassed by them.

Discipline

If you are tempted, enticed, or intrigued by the possible benefits immediate gratification may bring, you are human. If, however, you are weak of character and unable to resist temptations in your job, get out. I'm serious. You need to consider an alternate career because this one is not for you. There are too many good, decent, honest, and loyal officers across the country who put their lives at risk to make communities better, safer places to live. The parasites among them, the cowards who use and abuse the shield for corrupt purposes, need to go.

Crossing the Line

In life, there are lines: good vs. bad, right vs. wrong, ethical vs. unethical. Which side are you on? Give an example of each. Just write down the first thing that comes to your mind.

GOOD
_____
_____
_____

BAD
_____
_____
_____

RIGHT
_____
_____
_____

WRONG
_____
_____
_____

ETHICAL
_____
_____
_____

UNETHICAL
_____
_____
_____

Please review your list any time you feel uncertainty about a decision you are about to make. Some lines must never be crossed.

When an officer crosses the line, he or she is believed to have taken the path of dishonor and inappropriateness. Remember our earlier discussion about being held to a higher standard? An officer who crosses the line turns his or her back on the entire profession.

Throughout my years of studying, teaching, training, and researching, I have informally interviewed officers in hallways, in classrooms, in patrol cars, on the streets, and during lunches and have been both amazed and outraged. My amazement has come from the wonderful stories of courage, strength, hope, and professionalism told to me by so many. My outrage has come from the pathetic excuses for dishonor told to me, thankfully, by only a few.

Nevertheless, the many can learn from the few, so here is the "top 10" list, if you will, told to me during my years of research as rationales by those who wear (or wore) blue and who have crossed the line:

1. Easy to get away with it
2. Pressure
3. Money
4. No consequences
5. Need to fit in
6. Sex
7. Bad relationship with supervisor
8. Not enough pay
9. Others' bad examples
10. Marital troubles/divorce

Discuss each issue in class with your colleagues and instructor. Give your opinion about each one.

1. Easy to get away with it

_____

_____

_____

_____

_____

2. Pressure

_____

_____

_____

_____

_____

3. Money

_____

_____

_____

_____

4. No consequences

_____

_____

_____

_____

_____

5. Need to fit in

_____

_____

_____

_____

_____

6. Sex

_____

_____

_____

_____

_____

7. Bad relationship with supervisor

_____

_____

_____

_____

_____

8. Not enough pay

_____

_____

_____

_____

_____

9. Others' bad examples

_____

_____

_____

_____

_____

10. Marital troubles/divorce

_____

_____

_____

_____

_____

The Slippery Slope

If you step foot on a slippery slope, do you increase your odds of falling? This is like asking questions such as, if you drink alcohol, do you increase your odds of becoming an alcoholic? If you gamble, do you increase your odds (no pun intended) of developing out-of-control gambling behavior? If you speed, do you increase your odds of getting into an accident? The answer to all of these questions is a resounding yes!

The slippery slope theory is one that can be applied to any facet of human behavior. It is important to our discussion of ethics to explore four elements of this theory relative to how we conduct ourselves:

1. Free will
2. Involved participation
3. Appropriateness
4. Consequences

First, because we live in a free society, we are afforded the opportunity to move and think freely. I would like to present you with a case, a true example of police trainees who found themselves on the slippery slope and slid rapidly downward. After analyzing this scenario, let's look at the four elements of the theory.

Two police trainees, Rick and Dave, were one week shy of graduating from the police academy. They had successfully completed all classroom and practical areas of the training curriculum and were preparing to take the state certification exam. On a Saturday evening, at approximately 11:30 P.M., they decided to go to an exotic dance club, which featured ladies disrobing on stage. While at the club, they ordered several alcoholic drinks and were becoming increasingly loud and obnoxious. On two occasions, the manager told them to settle down. On the third occasion, the manager told them to leave, at which time Rick stood up, pushed the manager, and stated, "Shut the hell up, Asshole. We're cops!" The manager asked for ID. Dave took out a badge and asked, "OK, Shitface. Satisfied?" The manager went to his office and called the police. Shortly thereafter, the police arrived and arrested Rick for battery, intoxication, and impersonating an officer; Dave was arrested for intoxication and impersonating an officer. Their careers in law enforcement were over. Now, using this scenario, let's address the four elements of the slippery slope theory.

Free Will

Question: Did Rick and Dave exercise free will?
Answer: Yes

Which statements are true?

1. Rick and Dave decided to go to the exotic dance club.
2. Rick and Dave drank several alcoholic beverages.
3. Rick and Dave decided to get loud and obnoxious.
4. Rick pushed the manager.
5. Rick stated that they were cops.
6. Rick and Dave showed the manager their badges.
7. Rick and Dave were disrespectful to the manager.

As you review these statements, you will agree that all are *true* based on the facts of the case. Let's address the second element of the slippery slope theory.

Involved Participation

The slippery slope theory maintains that behaviors may quickly become increasingly worse, depending on the extent to which the participants are involved. In the Rick and Dave case, it appears as though both parties were *involved* in the following:

1. Drinking alcoholic beverages
2. Becoming loud and obnoxious
3. Using profanity
4. Impersonating an officer

What do you think would have happened if the two trainees had decided to go to the movies or to a football game instead? Chances are pretty good that they would have graduated from the Academy, passed the state certification exam, and started their careers in law enforcement. However, I must ask your opinion. Would this (or something similar) have happened, with far worse circumstances, down the road? Could be.

Appropriateness

Daily, each of us must examine the appropriateness of our behavior. An easy way to make this determination is to consider the following three areas:

1. *Status.* One's status (e.g., position, rank, title, professional affiliation) should be considered when deciding on places to go, people to associate with, and behavior to participate in.
2. *Time.* Is the time of day a factor for consideration regarding appropriateness? Yes. Different things may happen at 11:30 A.M. vs. 11:30 P.M. Right?
3. *Place.* Is the place one is planning to go (e.g., a bar, a church, the beach, a casino) an appropriate place given one's status? That's for you to decide.

Let's examine the last element of the slippery slope theory.

Consequences

The fourth element of the slippery slope theory involves consequences. Remember the saying, "Let your conscience be your guide." When analyzing ethics, if the consequences of potential actions appear stringent and potentially damaging to your health, safety, and career, let your conscience be your guide: Refrain.

By not stepping onto the slippery slope and taking the high road instead, you are using your most impressive weapon: your brain.

Discuss the four elements of the slippery slope theory in class:

1. Free will

_____

_____

_____

_____

_____

2. Involved participation

_____

_____

_____

_____

3. Appropriateness

_____

_____

_____

_____

_____

4. Consequences

_____

_____

_____

_____

_____

10 Types of Police Deviance

Gratuity

A gratuity is the receipt of free meals, services, or discounts. Some officers consider these fringe benefits of the job. Gratvities violate the Code of Ethics because they involve financial reward or gain, and they are corrupt because the officer has been placed in a compromising position where favors (a "fix") can be reasonably expected in the future. When there is an implied favor, it's a gratuity and should be avoided.

Gratuities often lead to things like kickbacks (bribery) for referring business to towing companies, ambulances, or garages. Along the unethical scale comes pilfering, or stealing a company's supplies for personal use. At the extreme, opportunistic theft takes place, when police officers "skim" items of value that won't be missed from crime scenes, property rooms, warehouses, or any place they have access to. Theft of items from stores while an officer is on patrol is called "shopping."

Shakedown

A shakedown is when the police extort a business owner for protection money. One example may involve gay bars, which are considered the most vulnerable. In some cities, police are still charged with the power to inspect bars. In other cities, officers may promise extra protection against gay-bashing in return for extra payments. In other cities, moonlighting officers would make extra money from establishments and be paid extra for overlooking sexual activity or drug violations.

Shakedowns are also common forms of deviance involving strip bars, prostitution rings, drug dealing, illegal gambling, and even construction projects.

Perjury

This is usually a means to affect a particular outcome of a circumstance, such as when an officer leaves out certain pertinent information in order to "fix" a criminal prosecution. When officers lie to protect other officers, a cycle of deviance occurs that often leads to many other lies and forms of deception.

Brutality

Brutality takes several forms such as excessive force, name calling, sarcasm, ridicule, disrespect, and violence that does not support a legitimate police function.

Examples may include forms of:

■ Profane or abusive language
■ Disrespectful commands to move or go home
■ Unwarranted field stops and searches
■ Threats of implied violence
■ Prodding with a nightstick or approaching with a pistol
■ The actual use of physical force that supercedes the action

Profanity

As public servants, police officers should communicate professionally and avoid profanity.

Types of profanity that are discouraged include:

■ Words having religious connotations
■ Words indicating excretory functions
■ Words connected with sexual functions

Use of such language by police officers is intentional and not a loss of control, but rather used:

- To gain the attention of citizens who may be less than cooperative
- To discredit somebody or something, such as an alibi defense
- To establish a dominant–submissive relationship
- To identify with an in-group, the offender or police subculture
- To label or degrade a group

Sex on Duty or Duty-Related

Situations involving this type of behavior include:

- Traffic stops — to get a closer look at the female or information about her
- Fox hunting — stopping college girls to get to know them
- Voyeurism — window peeping or interrupting couples during intimacy
- Victim contacts — consoling victims who have psychological needs
- Opposite-sex strip searches — touching and/or sex with jail inmates
- Sexual shakedowns — letting prostitutes go if they perform sex acts

Sleeping on Duty

Sleeping on duty, of course, is an extreme example of avoiding or performing only the amount minimally necessary to satisfy superiors. Avoidance of duty can take many forms: from ignoring or passing on calls for service to someone else, overlooking suspicious behavior, or engaging in personal business while on duty.

Drinking and Abusing Drugs

The potential for officers to abuse alcohol or drugs is high. The officer usually obtains the drugs from some intermediary, involves others in transactions, and opens the door to blackmail, shakedowns, rip-offs, and cover-ups. It sets a bad example for public relations. It will affect judgment and lead to greater likelihood of deadly force or traffic accidents. Alcohol and drug use tend to become a systemic problem: others become involved, either supporting or condemning the user. Alcohol and drugs tend to be mixed by police officers because there's more subcultural support for alcoholism, thus the abuser covers up the drug use with alcoholism.

More intriguing is when police officers become sellers or dealers of drugs. The motivation here appears to be monetary gain and greed, attempting to claim stress or undercover assignments as a defense.

Misuse of Confidential Information

This normally involves the jeopardization of an ongoing investigation by "leaking" information to friends, relatives, the public, the press, or in some cases, directly to the criminal suspects or members of a gang. In other cases, department resources, such as computer systems, may be used to produce criminal history reports for "friends."

Willful Neglect of Duty

Simply not responding to calls for service is unacceptable. Some reasons cited as to why officers engage in this type of deviance are because they:

- Have an ax to grind with supervisors, colleagues, or the department, so this type of behavior is seen as a way for them to "get back at" the system.
- Are nearing retirement and want to take it easy toward the end of their career.
- Fear their surroundings (some officers shy away from calls they know involve drug deals, crime suspects, or perceived hostile environments).
- Feel nothing will be done, even if they respond to the call (e.g., prostitution, gambling, and juvenile delinquency).

Certainly, as a sworn officer you are involved in a wide variety of activities, to include:

- Controlling politically motivated riots.
- Dealing with cases of assault.
- Investigating murders.
- Intervening in domestic and neighborhood disputes.
- Apprehending suspects.
- Saving people's lives.
- Making drug-related arrests.
- Shooting armed robbers.
- Dealing with cases of fraud, to name a few.

Therefore, you have a number of different important roles. You have a deterrence role as a highly visible authority figure with the right to deploy force. You also have a law enforcement role in relation to crimes that are already committed. You also have important preventive and social work roles. Therefore, your job is about ensuring the protection of basic moral rights, including the right to life, liberty, physical and property security. The overall outcome or goal of policing is the protection of constitutional rights. When you act in accordance with the legal, ethical principles of your profession, you achieve three things at the same time: You do what is morally right, your actions are lawful, and you act in accordance with the expectations of the community you serve.

Thank you for thinking about these important matters. Let's proceed to our next topic.

2

An Ethics Discussion

"Is it OK for an officer to accept free coffee, food, and other stuff?" asked the inquisitive trainee. The answer to this question has been debated for years and will continue to be argued for years to come.

In order to provide an appropriate response to this often-asked question, we need to analyze the definition of the term *ethics. Ethics means principles or accepted rules of conduct for a particular individual or group as mandated by law, policy, or procedure.* Let's examine each component of this definition of ethics and begin our discussion.

Principles or Accepted Rules of Conduct

Almost everything in life is based on rules. Sports enthusiasts are familiar with the rules of football. When a player is cited for an illegal face mask, he has broken an important rule of the game and will incur a penalty. That penalty may adversely impact him as well as his teammates. At the Academy, a trainee who violates an institutional rule may find himself or herself facing counseling, a reprimand, or stringent disciplinary action. At the police or corrections department, an officer who does not adhere to the rules may encounter unwanted media attention, liability, and possibly termination. Therefore, it's fair to say that a significant consequence may act as a deterrent for future inappropriate behavior. However, if no consequence exists or if the consequence is not enforced, the rule breaker may be inspired to continue along a path of inappropriate conduct.

For a Particular Individual or Group

Doctors, lawyers, accountants, police officers, and many others have something in common. These professionals have strict guidelines they must adhere to in order to maintain their certifications. Professionals of this caliber are held to high standards, and each group member has a unique ethical code to which he or she must comply. Failure to comply may result in decertification.

As Mandated by Law, Policy, or Procedure

When something is in writing, we notice it, read it, refer to it, remember it, and ultimately *adhere* to it. Therefore, if criminal justice directors, administrators, trainers, practitioners, and educators are serious about *enforcing ethics*, they must work collaboratively to implement specific state (and even federal) guidelines that police and corrections departments must follow. Additionally, department representatives could reinforce these guidelines by writing policies and procedures that explain, clearly and completely, the behaviors that will and will not be tolerated for officers representing their police or corrections departments.

The following illustration easily could be added to a department's standard operating procedures under the ethics category. The following behaviors are unacceptable and are viewed by this department as unethical:

1. Accepting gratuities (e.g., gifts, favors, money, or anything given to you *free*)
2. Using unnecessary force (e.g., physical abuse, emotional mistreatment, or roughing up suspects in custody)
3. Discriminating (mistreating individuals on the basis of race, age, gender, religion, culture, sexual preference, or national origin)
4. Lying in any form (including creating facts to incriminate or protect another)
5. Violating laws, rights, or procedures (e.g., intentionally making a false arrest, filing a false report, or purposely ignoring departmental procedures)

Add five more unacceptable behaviors to this list:

6. _____

_____

7. _____

_____

8. _____

_____

9. _____

_____

10. _____

_____

Remember, if you put it in writing, officers will listen and respond accordingly!

Another point of interest that addresses this discussion is the meaning of the term *gratuity*. *A gratuity is something of value given to another because of that person's status or role.* Usually, when a gratuity is offered, the receiver and giver benefit.

An officer should consider the following questions when deciding whether a gratuity is being offered:

1. Why is this individual offering me this?
2. Is this individual offering me this because I am an officer?
3. If I were not an officer, would this individual offer me this?
4. Ethically, what should I do?

In answering the trainee's question about "free coffee, food, and other stuff," we can use the four-question approach to reach an appropriate answer:

Question 1: Why is this individual offering me this?

Answer 1: Unless you, the officer, straightforwardly ask the store owner or manager the question why, you can only guess the answer. Maybe the store owner sincerely appreciates your service. Maybe he wants you to be visible in his store to deter would-be perpetrators. Maybe he wants you to fix a ticket he received.

Question 2: Is this individual offering me this because I am an officer?

Answer 2: Yes.

Question 3: If I were not an officer, would this individual offer me this?

Answer 3: No.

Question 4: Ethically, what should I do?

Answer 4: Ethically, you should respectfully decline a citizen's offer of *free* anything. I am not suggesting that the officer who accepts a free cup of coffee is walking the path of corruption and deception. I am suggesting that power and authority are involved here. Officers are powerful people. Some become blinded by this; others do not. Some begin to expect and accept things; others expect and accept nothing. Remain humble and honest. Expect one thing: the paycheck you earned ethically.

Now that we are on our way to understanding ethics, we need to explore some of the factors that contribute to questionable conduct among police and corrections professionals. At the end of the workbook, we will analyze possible solutions to prevent unethical conduct within the criminal justice field.

3

Contributing Factors

In order for us to understand what causes an officer to cross the line and behave inappropriately, we need to recognize some of the factors that contribute to *why* an officer may behave a certain way in the first place. The following acronym will pinpoint key areas of this discussion:

E—Environment
T—Training Academy
H—Home Life
I—Individual Beliefs
C—Citizens
S—Stress

Environment

First, the officer's *environment* is going to affect his or her attitudes, beliefs, and actions. Allow me to introduce you to two brothers: Charles and Chris. Both men grew up in a hostile neighborhood. Gangs were prevalent, drug dealing was common, and violent criminal conduct was a nearly daily occurrence. The brothers' parents worked diligently and legitimately to provide their children with as much as they could afford: a roof over their heads, food in their stomachs, and clothes on their backs. Overall, it wasn't easy, but they managed. As the brothers grew up, their relationship grew apart, as did their interests. Charles went to Penn State and Chris went to the State Pen. Why did one choose education and the other incarceration? Did their environment have something to do with it? Maybe something, but not everything.

Let's meet two officers: Officer George and Officer Allen. Both officers went through the Academy together. They struggled through defensive tactics, legal studies, and report writing. They made it, and now both are sworn officers in different departments. Officer George is on the fast track to the top of the success ladder. He has established an impressive reputation within the department. His colleagues regard him as a cop's cop, and the citizens in his patrol neighborhood have written letters of commendation on his behalf. When asked about his work ethic, Officer George responds, "I'm in a great squad. The sarge is supportive, we know what we need to do, and we do it as a team. I love what I do, and I want to make the department proud." Officer Allen's approach to his position, unfortunately, is quite different from his colleague's. Officer Allen arrives late to work on numerous occasions. He has started drinking alcohol heavily after his shift, and he has had several complaints filed against him for discourteous conduct. When asked about his work ethic, Officer Allen responds, "This department is the worst. We've got tension so thick here you can cut it with a chain saw. There's no support, no unity. We've got religious cliques, ethnic issues, and a total lack of caring. The citizens don't help us. They hate us. So what do they expect from me? To be honest, I don't give a sh—!"

What went wrong along the way to distort this picture? We have two young officers who started their careers in law enforcement with enthusiasm and vigor. Now, one is committed to service and the other is cynical about serving. Is their working environment a factor? Yes. It's not an excuse, nor is it the only piece to this puzzle. However, the working environment in which the officer finds himself or herself will impact his or her tendency to succeed and thrive or to succumb and falter. Behavior is contagious. When we associate with officers who are upbeat and energetic, we tend to respond to situations in a similar manner. However, when we are in a day-to-day relationship with those who are lethargic and apathetic, we too may find ourselves taking on similar traits. Although we cannot always control our work environment, we can control our actions and reactions at home, on the street, at the department, and at the Academy.

Training Academy

What role does the *Training Academy* play in shaping a recruit's ethics? The Academy plays a tremendous part in how a trainee interacts with fellow colleagues, supervisors, and instructors. One of the most important steps a Training Center can take in encouraging appropriate behavior is to have, in writing, a Trainee Code of

Conduct. The Code should address areas that trainees must remain mindful of on a daily basis while at the Basic Training Academy.

The following example illustrates a sample code that an Academy may want to adopt:

We, the administrators, faculty, and staff of _____ _____ Training Institute, expect trainees at this School to adhere to these standards:

1. To meet the rigorous academic challenges of this institution.
2. To communicate respectfully and professionally, at all times, with every person with whom they come in contact.
3. To complete assignments and examinations in a timely, honest, and efficient manner (cheating of any kind is strictly prohibited).
4. To exhibit pride in being part of a unique learning opportunity.
5. To remain alert and inquisitive while classroom discussions are taking place.
6. To arrive promptly for every class session.
7. To enthusiastically carry out orders given to them by staff members.
8. To seek counsel from the appropriate staff member(s) when matters of a personal nature arise.
9. To support fellow Academy recruits in their pursuit of excellence.
10. To report any inappropriate behavior on the part of another trainee, instructor, or officer to the respective command staff.

When individuals are given clear and reasonable written expectations, more often than not, they comply.

Additionally, Academy instructors play a significant role in shaping and reinforcing the manner in which a trainee interacts with others. Some believe experience is the best teacher. Others say we learn best when we mirror the behavior of well-educated professional individuals who teach us through their actions. Perhaps it's a combination of both. As we analyze the role of the Academy instructor, whose goal is to teach job-related conduct as well as to encourage ethical ways of thinking and behaving, many would agree these fine instructors share the following traits:

■ *Professionalism.* Professional instructors take pride in themselves and view the classroom environment as a teaching and learning experience for all. These individuals encourage questions in class, praise effort and achievement, and strive to bring out the best in their students. Professional instructors adhere to a "firm but fair" model. They are aware, at all times, of what they say and the manner in which they say it. They do not use threatening or demeaning tactics. When critique of another's action is warranted, they address the wrongfulness of the act and encourage the trainee to provide solutions as well as to learn from the experience. The best Academy instructors are mentors, role models, and people whose conduct should be praised and emulated.

- *Expertise.* Training Centers have an enormous task at hand when it comes to ensuring that all trainees meet the learning objectives consistent with state certification requirements. Therefore, every instructor must possess a high degree of skill, knowledge, and experience in his or her instructional field. Whether the instructor is a full-time or part-time employee, students can distinguish those who are knowledgeable from those who pretend to be.

- *Preparation.* Officers are expected to be fully prepared each day for work. They are trained to handle the emotional, physical, and intellectual demands a work shift may bring. Their tools are readily available at all times: handcuffs, notebook, and intellect. The Academy instructor must be prepared to instruct each time he or she enters a classroom. The lesson plan should address the training topic for that day. All handouts must be clearly written and organized. Trainees don't want instructors to "wing it." Students deserve better than that. Do we want officers to "wing it" on the streets or at a corrections facility? No! Preparation is essential.

- *CPR: Courtesy, Professionalism, and Respect.* If we want trainees to conduct themselves in a respectful manner while at the Academy and in the field, *all* training personnel should show them how it's done by behaving courteously, professionally, and respectfully to one another. There are many messages (some subtle and others not) that instructors and staff communicate to the trainees. The training environment must be based on neutrality. Learning simply cannot take place in an atmosphere that allows discrimination or harassment. Therefore, comments, jokes, or slurs of an inappropriate, offensive nature must be prohibited.

Clearly, the Training Center plays a part in shaping how a criminal justice professional may behave while at the Academy, on the streets, or at the corrections facility. What else affects the manner in which an officer chooses to act?

Home Life

Although the physical structure of some homes may appear similar, *home life* (what goes on behind closed doors) will vary from one household to the next.

When we examine the topic of ethics as it relates to police and corrections officers, we need to take a look at the officer's former and present home life.

First, do the parents of officers play a part in shaping how an officer looks at the world and responds to various conditions? Of course they do! Not every officer was raised in a traditional two-parent household. Maybe the officer was raised by one parent, a grandparent, or a caring guardian. Whatever the case may be, many children raised in law enforcement households respect their parents' professions and choose to follow in similar footsteps by seeking employment opportunities in the criminal justice field.

What if an officer's parents instilled in him or her as a child a lack of tolerance for those who are different? Ultimately, this type of early belief system will impact one's thinking as an adult. What if an officer's parents instilled in him or her a healthy respect toward diverse populations? Chances are the officer will grow up interacting well with those who are unique in their own right, as dissimilar as they may appear to be to the officer.

Although the parents of officers are a part of the whole picture, we cannot point accusatory fingers at them. At some point in an officer's young adult life, he or she will start formulating opinions and behaving as he or she *chooses* to behave. Therefore, regardless of what their mom, dad, grandpa, or guardian once said, officers will make up their own minds about how to behave in different settings and under various circumstances.

Does the officer's present home life affect his or her job-related conduct? Yes, it does! An officer's home life usually fits into one of three categories: living at home with parents, living alone or with a roommate, or living with a spouse. The common thread that weaves its way into an officer's personal life, which affects his or her professional life, is the *emotional support* of a significant other. For purposes of this discussion, the term *significant other* refers to a parent, roommate, girlfriend, boyfriend, or spouse. An important question an officer should ask himself or herself is this: "Does my significant other support my role as an officer?" If the answer is yes, the officer usually experiences peace of mind. If the answer is no, interpersonal conflict may occur at some point. Clearly, friction at home could lead to ethical concerns on the job.

Another important theme regarding an officer's home life and how it affects the officer's ethics is loyalty to his or her spouse. Some research studies suggest officers are at risk of experiencing marital problems when compared to other professionals. The following five factors have been cited as contributing to the breakup of an officer's marriage:

1. Lack of time spent at home
2. Secretive demeanor
3. Alcohol use
4. Adultery
5. Consuming interest in career

Officer, do you want to be happily married? If so, like anything else, it takes hard work, dedication, and a willingness to compromise!

To maintain a loyal, committed, and lasting marriage, officers should consider the following 10 ethical home rules:

Rule 1.   *Communicate honestly with one another.* When you have had a lousy day and you feel your emotions have been through the wringer, talk it out. Too often, too many spouses of officers find their partners in life drifting away from them. Drift is a two-way process. If one starts to drift, the other must pull the partner back to solid marital ground. Being secretive and keeping your emotions bottled up inside can do more damage than good. Talk it out; don't burn out.

Rule 2.   *Discuss expectations.* Unless an individual is a gifted mind reader, it is virtually impossible to know what one spouse expects from the other until important issues are discussed. What are the financial expectations? Who is expected to help the kids with homework? Who cooks dinner and attends to household duties? Negotiation is the key to understanding and meeting another's reasonable expectations.

Rule 3.   *Wear different hats.* An officer must wear different hats to meet the demands of the profession. One minute you're a psychologist, the next minute a legal scholar, and the next a medical responder. You need to be able to take off your "work hat" and put on your "home hat." Maybe that means being a mom or dad, maybe it means being a lover or friend, or maybe it means being a person who is relaxed with and supportive of those you care about.

Rule 4.   *Work it out.* Every marriage has its bumpy road. For some couples, "for worse" lasts longer than they had hoped. The partners who make it through trying times certainly can appreciate the meaning of togetherness and teamwork. At times, a couple may seek counseling from a skilled third-party professional. Ultimately, a meaningful marriage is quite similar to an exercise program: With effort, consistency, and a "don't quit" attitude, positive results can be achieved.

Rule 5.   *Have fun.* Arrange a dinner or lunch date with your spouse. Plan a weekend getaway together. Go bike riding. Do the things you used to do before the pressures of your occupation set in.

Rule 6.   *Be willing to compromise.* Some people believe that a marriage is (or is supposed to be) 50/50. Well, not necessarily. Sometimes a marriage needs to be 60/40, 70/30, or even 90/10 for it to survive. It depends upon what phase the marriage is in. Perhaps one partner is ill and needs more attention than usual. Maybe a child is going through a difficult time at school and requires both of you to help her. Compromise as a *couple!*

Rule 7.   *Capture lasting memories.* It's nice to sit down with couples who have been together a long time. They reminisce about when they were teenagers, in their 20s, 40s, etc. and smile lovingly as they recount special times together. A lasting memory may be a renewal of your wedding vows, the birth of your first child, or your promotion to a higher rank.

Rule 8.   *Do things as a couple and as an individual.* As we know, an officer's work shift is not as traditional as that of a doctor's, lawyer's, or accountant's. Therefore, make time, even at nontraditional times, to do nice things together as a couple. It is also very important that you articulate to your spouse your need of a little *alone* time. If your wife wants you to go with her to the ballet, or to a concert, or to the mall, go! If you want to play golf, work out at the gym, or jog—go!

Rule 9.   *Keep it light.* It is very likely that if you are an officer anywhere in the United States, you experience more stress than the average professional. The ability to "keep it light" at home means that your spouse, children, in-laws, and friends are not the same as (and should not be treated as) defendants, suspects, or victims. Maintaining a "light" perspective rather than a "heavy" one about day-to-day family matters will be good for your heart, your family, and your marriage.

Rule 10.   *Make financial plans.* It is very important to plan for a secure financial future. Even if you are a young officer, consider the importance of financial planning, investing, and saving. Many times, marriages fall apart because couples live well beyond their economic means and buy, buy, buy. They forget about save, save, save! You'd be surprised how investing a little bit each pay period may add up to quite a lucrative sum for your family to enjoy for a happy, healthy retirement!

List five more ethical home rules officers could follow to make their relationships positive and lasting:

Rule 11.   _____

_____

_____

_____

Rule 12. _____

_____

_____

_____

Rule 13. _____

_____

_____

_____

Rule 14. _____

_____

_____

_____

Rule 15. _____

_____

_____

_____

Individual Beliefs

Another factor influencing an officer's behavior is his or her *individual beliefs*. When an officer treats citizens with respect and dignity, it is because the officer believes human beings deserve to be treated with respect and dignity. If an officer treats suspects in an abusive, brutal manner, it is because the officer believes this method of treatment is acceptable and justifiable. If an officer crosses the line, it is because he or she believes the opportunity exists to do so. Down the road, you may be provoked by an intoxicated subject, an intimidating colleague, or the lure of a quick, easy buck. Officer, be ready to maintain your control and stand for something; otherwise, you risk falling for anything! So, who influences an officer's individual beliefs? Many people contribute to an officer's views of the world: family members, instructors, friends, supervisors, colleagues, clergy, citizens, and the media. Although others may be influential, ultimately an officer believes what he or she chooses to believe.

It is important for officers to individually and collectively believe in certain fundamental principles. The following list represents five universal beliefs of ethical officers:

Officers' Ethical Beliefs

1. As an officer, I believe in the constitutional rights of all people.
2. As an officer, I believe in providing the best service of which I am capable at all times.
3. As an officer, I believe in conducting myself, on and off duty, with pride and professionalism.
4. As an officer, I believe in obeying the laws of the state and the policies of my department.
5. As an officer, I believe in treating people fairly and without favoritism or bias.

Add five more ethical beliefs to this list:

6. As an officer, I believe _____

_____

_____

7. As an officer, I believe _____

_____

_____

8. As an officer, I believe _____

_____

_____

9. As an officer, I believe _____

_____

_____

10. As an officer, I believe _____

_____

_____

Citizens

You promised to protect and serve the *citizens* of your community. Unfortunately, some of these men and women may not abide by the laws, and some may not regard favorably what you represent: power, authority, and compliance. Therefore, when an officer finds himself or herself, day after day, patrolling a neighborhood in which negative feelings for law enforcement are pervasive, it's certainly challenging for the officer to view the people in a positive light.

It would be advantageous to the community and the department for administrators to allow their police and corrections colleagues time during a work shift to participate in community-oriented projects.

Let's analyze five ways in which police and corrections officers could improve the perception citizens have of them:

1. Officers could attend neighborhood crime watch meetings on a regular basis.
2. Officers could meet with elementary, middle school, high school, and college classes to explain the wide range of skills police and corrections officers need to be effective.
3. Officers could volunteer to coach Little League games or teach elderly people how to be safe.
4. Officers could get to know the names of residents and local merchants in their community.
5. Officers could prepare meals or collect toys for those who are less fortunate.

List five more ways officers could improve their relations with citizens:

6. _____

_____

_____

7. _____

_____

_____

8. _____

_____

_____

9. _____

_____

_____

10. _____

_____

Stress

Thus far, we have discussed various factors that contribute to an officer's decision to behave ethically or unethically. Does *stress* play a part in how officers conduct themselves?

Absolutely! The term *stress* refers to a physical or emotional reaction to a condition or situation. Perhaps now, more than ever, criminal justice professionals are stressed out! Why? Because practically everybody—citizens, supervisors, and the media—is watching the moves they make. Therefore, if reactions and behaviors are not managed effectively, officers may find themselves or their colleagues acting inappropriately. Although it is unrealistic to believe that life is, or even should be, completely stress-free, it is realistic to examine situations that contribute to stress for officers. Additionally, we will explore warning signs of stress as well as positive measures that can be taken to adapt to difficult conditions. Remember, you can react well to your surroundings, even under adverse situations, and you can conduct yourself ethically.

Experts maintain that the following twelve situations are stressful:

1. Death of a loved one (spouse, family member, close friend)
2. Divorce
3. Termination from employment
4. Serious injury or illness
5. Incarceration in jail or prison
6. Separation from marital partner
7. Financial problems
8. Promotion at work
9. Retirement
10. Marriage
11. Testing
12. Court appearance

What's interesting about this list is that some of the situations are positive (promotion, retirement, marriage, and testing). Therefore, even when good things happen to us, we may still be faced with pressure. What are some of the signs officers should look for to determine if they or their colleagues are experiencing stress? The following table illustrates physical and emotional symptoms (ranging from severe to high to medium to low):

PHYSICAL SYMPTOMS		EMOTIONAL SYMPTOMS	
Severe	Heart attack Ulcers	**Severe**	Suicidal thoughts Striking others Frequent outbursts of temper
High	Heart palpitations Vomiting	**High**	Depression Blaming others Anger

Medium	Frequent colds	**Medium**	Use of alcohol to unwind
	Nervousness		Loss of enthusiasm
	Upset stomach		
Low	Facial tension	**Low**	Lack of energy
	Headaches		Worrying

It is essential for you, as police and corrections professionals, to be able to manage your responses and reactions to various conditions so that you will be effective and healthy representatives of your departments. Experts recommend the following 10 stress-management techniques:

1. Breathe deeply.
2. Exercise regularly.
3. Eat nutritious foods.
4. Get enough rest.
5. Talk about feelings.
6. Listen to music.
7. Write about feelings.
8. Plan for the future.
9. Laugh a lot.
10. Participate in enjoyable activities.

List five more things you can do to effectively handle stressful situations:

11. _____

_____

_____

12. _____

_____

_____

13. _____

_____

_____

14. _____

_____

_____

15. _____

_____

_____

Now that we have explored six factors that influence an officer's decision to behave ethically or not, it's time for you and your colleagues to read and discuss thought-provoking ethics-related scenarios in the next chapter, titled Ethical Encounters. Compare your responses to your colleagues' responses.

4

Ethical Encounters

Scenario 1

THE CLUB SANDWICH

This is your first week on the job as a newly sworn police officer. You performed well in all of your classes at the Academy. You particularly enjoyed the ethics class. You found the scenarios interesting, and you made a promise to yourself that you would never accept freebies or act in a manner unbecoming to the profession. On this day, you and two senior officers clear a lunch break with the dispatcher. You enjoy a pleasant lunch: a club sandwich. After the meal, your fellow officers get up to leave as you reach for your wallet. One officer asks, "What are you doing?" You respond, "I'm paying for my lunch." He says, "Kid, it's on the house. That's why we eat here." You respond, "At the Academy, we were taught accepting discounted or free meals is unethical." Both officers laugh and say, "Kid, forget the Academy. This is the real world."

Ethically, what should you do?

_____

_____

_____

_____

_____

_____

_____

_____

_____

_____

_____

_____

Scenario 2

THE PERJURER

You and your partner are dispatched to a robbery call. The dispatcher describes the suspect as a white male juvenile, approximately 15 to 17 years of age, wearing a black T-shirt, blue jeans, and tennis shoes. A few blocks east of the scene, your partner sees someone who fits the suspect's description. Your partner exits the patrol car and shouts, "Police! Stop!" The juvenile starts running, and your partner runs after him. Moments later, your partner fires his revolver, shooting the juvenile in the back. You call rescue. They respond and transport the juvenile to the hospital. Meanwhile, your partner takes you aside and says, "I need you to back me. You gotta help me. No matter who asks, tell them it *looked* like the kid was about to draw a weapon." (The truth is, the juvenile did not have a weapon.) Later that day, Officer Thomas from Internal Affairs asks you to tell him what happened.

Ethically, what should you do?

_____

_____

_____

_____

_____

_____

_____

_____

_____

_____

_____

_____

Scenario 3

THE FALSE REPORT

You and a senior officer are on routine patrol. You come across a juvenile whom you have repeatedly seen in and out of court. You personally know him to have been involved in a total of six property crimes. You are tired of seeing him go through the "revolving door" of justice. Your partner suggests you file a false report on him. After all, the kid's "got to pay" for his actions. Right?

Ethically, what should you do?

_____

_____

_____

_____

_____

_____

_____

_____

_____

_____

_____

_____

_____

_____

_____

Scenario 4

The Favor

You are a corrections officer who works in a maximum-security facility. Yesterday, you misplaced your keys. Fortunately, Inmate Jones found your keys, and he returned them to you. Tonight, he tells you he received a letter from his wife, who is filing for divorce. He asks you if he can use the phone to call her. He already used the phone earlier today, and it is now "lights out."

Ethically, what should you do?

_____

_____

_____

_____

_____

_____

_____

_____

_____

_____

_____

_____

_____

_____

_____

_____

Scenario 5

THE PROMOTIONAL TEST

You are studying for the promotional test to become a sergeant. You do not have a lot of time throughout the day to study. A friend of yours, a sergeant, says that he has a sample copy of the exam. You know that sample copies are forbidden.

Ethically, what should you do?

_____

_____

_____

_____

_____

_____

_____

_____

_____

_____

_____

_____

_____

_____

_____

_____

Scenario 6

THE MONEY

You are a newly promoted lieutenant in the Narcotics Division of the bureau. While standing at the water fountain, you overhear two of your colleagues, Sergeants Jay Anderson and Dan Foster, discussing last night's $7,500 drug bust. According to the property report, $5,000 was seized. What happened to the $2,500?

Ethically, what should you do?

_____

_____

_____

_____

_____

_____

_____

_____

_____

_____

_____

_____

_____

_____

_____

_____

Scenario 7

THE CHEATER

Today, you received the results of the sergeant's promotional exam. You devoted a great deal of time to studying. The two officers with the highest score get promoted. You received a score of 94 percent. Officer Perez received a score of 95 percent and Officer Davis received a score of 96 percent. You saw Officer Perez refer to hand-written notes during the administration of the test. (Notes are forbidden.) You never told anyone about this.

Ethically, what should you do?

_____

_____

_____

_____

_____

_____

_____

_____

_____

_____

_____

_____

_____

_____

_____

_____

Scenario 8

THE WALLET

You are an off-duty officer who has just completed a three-mile run. You decide to cool off and rest under a big oak tree. You sit down under the tree and see a brown leather wallet close by. Curiosity gets the best of you, and you open the wallet. Interestingly enough, you find credit cards, identification, and $300 in cash. Nobody else is around.

Ethically, what should you do? What if you found $3,000, $30,000, or more?

_____

_____

_____

_____

_____

_____

_____

_____

_____

_____

_____

_____

_____

_____

Scenario 9

THE SUPERVISOR

You are a newly promoted sergeant appointed to the Communications Bureau of your department. You supervise six people. During the past several weeks, you have observed laziness among five of the six officers: arriving late to work, leaving work early, having long personal telephone conversations, and reading the newspaper. The lieutenant has told you to overlook "small stuff" and to give the guys "a break."

Ethically, what should you do?

_____

_____

_____

_____

_____

_____

_____

_____

_____

_____

_____

_____

_____

_____

_____

_____

_____

_____

Scenario 10

THE HARASSER

You are a probationary police officer. In two weeks, you will be on permanent status with your department. Your immediate supervisor, Sergeant Richards, repeatedly makes inappropriate comments to your colleague, a female probationary police officer regarding her "beautiful face" and "knock-out figure." This morning, you overhear Sergeant Richards tell her, "If you don't go out with me, you'll *never* make it past your probationary stage." She decides to file a report.

Ethically, what should you do?

_____

_____

_____

_____

_____

_____

_____

_____

_____

_____

_____

_____

_____

_____

Scenario 11

THE WHISTLE BLOWER

You are a corrections officer who is of high moral character and held in high esteem. Your colleagues and supervisors respect you, and they regard you as a team player. Today, you overhear two corrections officers discussing their "operation." Apparently, they are allowing inmates to receive narcotics and paraphernalia in the mail. The inmates are paying the officers for "looking the other way."

Ethically, what should you do?

_____

_____

_____

_____

_____

_____

_____

_____

_____

_____

_____

_____

_____

_____

_____

_____

Scenario 12

THE TRUTH

You are a 17-year veteran police officer, and you love the work you do. Your nephew just turned 21 years of age. He's as close as a son to you. Throughout his entire life, he listened attentively to your police stories and repeatedly commented, "I want to be just like you when I grow up. I want to be a cop." Now that he's of age, he has started the paperwork process, and he is interviewing with several police departments. The one flaw your nephew has is that he was an occasional drug user during adolescence. Despite this, he's a good kid and, in your opinion, would make a fine cop. He asks you if he should mention his past drug usage during upcoming interviews with prospective departments.

Ethically, what should you do?

_____

_____

_____

_____

_____

_____

_____

_____

_____

_____

_____

_____

_____

_____

Scenario 13

THE HOLIDAY GIFT

It's Christmas time, and the citizens in your patrol neighborhood are feeling festive and joyful. Jerry, the owner of Big Jerry's Grill, a well-known diner you frequently eat at, is having a holiday party tonight. Your sergeant tells you to drop by to make sure things are running smoothly. When Jerry sees you, he says, "You know, I really appreciate the work you do. Happy holidays!" He hands you a crisp $100 bill.

Ethically, what should you do?

_____

_____

_____

_____

_____

_____

_____

_____

_____

_____

_____

_____

_____

_____

_____

Scenario 14

THE CADET

You are a newly promoted lieutenant assigned to the Training Bureau of your department. One of the cadets in a basic training class has been reprimanded for the third time for unprofessional conduct. According to the standard operating procedures of your department, "Any cadet who receives three reprimands is to be terminated upon notice." This cadet happens to be a well-known politician's son.

Ethically, what should you do?

_____

_____

_____

_____

_____

_____

_____

_____

_____

_____

_____

_____

_____

_____

Scenario 15

THE AGGRESSOR

During a routine patrol with your colleague, Officer Ward, you observe a car traveling 40 mph (10 mph above the posted speed limit). Officer Ward pulls the car over. The driver, a 16-year-old female, produces her driver's license and registration. You hear Officer Ward say, "You women are all the same. If I pull you over again, I'm giving you a ticket." The next day, the driver and her mother meet with your captain, and they file a complaint against Officer Ward for "discourteous conduct." The captain asks you what happened.

Ethically, what should you do?

_____

_____

_____

_____

_____

_____

_____

_____

_____

_____

_____

_____

_____

_____

_____

_____

Scenario 16

THE BROTHER-IN-LAW

While on routine patrol, you observe a driver weaving in and out of three lanes of traffic. You notify the dispatcher that you are going to stop the vehicle. When you approach the passenger side of the vehicle, you are surprised to see the driver: your brother-in-law, Rick. Rick's eyes are bloodshot, his speech is slurred, and his breath smells of an unknown alcoholic beverage. When he sees you, he says, "Wow, man, am I glad to see you and not some other cop."

Ethically, what should you do?

_____

_____

_____

_____

_____

_____

_____

_____

_____

_____

_____

_____

_____

_____

_____

_____

Scenario 17

THE "PROFESSIONAL COURTESY" APPROACH

During your morning shift, you observe a motorist traveling 30 mph in a 15 mph school zone. You stop the vehicle, and the motorist immediately identifies himself as a corrections officer from the county. You decide to use "professional courtesy." You do not issue him a ticket.
     Is "professional courtesy" ethical?

_____

_____

_____

_____

_____

_____

_____

_____

_____

_____

_____

_____

_____

_____

_____

_____

_____

Scenario 18

THE DINNER BREAK

You and your partner have just cleared a dinner break with the dispatcher. It's been a rough shift: one burglary call in progress and a robbery. You and your partner finally sit down in a comfortable booth. You order a juicy steak dinner from the local barbecue restaurant. Shortly after your order arrives and you start eating, an elderly woman approaches you and says, "Officer, I locked my keys in my car."

Ethically, what should you do?

_____

_____

_____

_____

_____

_____

_____

_____

_____

_____

_____

_____

_____

_____

Scenario 19

THE CRANK CALL

It's Halloween! Throughout the day, at the top of each hour, a call comes in to the department regarding a shooting. Each officer who checks the alleged shootings finds them to be untrue. Throughout the day, 11 shooting-related calls have come in. The clock has just struck midnight. A caller reports a shooting and says it's an emergency.

Ethically, what should you do?

_____

_____

_____

_____

_____

_____

_____

_____

_____

_____

_____

_____

_____

_____

_____

Scenario 20

THE SKIMMER

Officer Burton, a 22-year veteran of the department, has been assigned to the Narcotics Division for the last eight years. Here and there, he "skims a little off the top." He justifies his behavior by saying, "After 22 years of busting my butt, I'm entitled to more than what they're paying me."

Is Officer Burton's behavior justifiable?

_____

_____

_____

_____

_____

_____

_____

_____

_____

_____

_____

_____

_____

_____

_____

_____

_____

Scenario 21

The Freebie

For the past several months, you have been stopping by the same convenience store in your patrol area to purchase gum, soda, and potato chips. Last week, a new owner purchased the store. During one of your work breaks, you walk in and the new owner says, "Officer, how nice to see you. Feel free to help yourself to anything you want. You guys do one helluva job."

Ethically, what should you do?

_____

_____

_____

_____

_____

_____

_____

_____

_____

_____

_____

_____

_____

_____

_____

Scenario 22

THE LATE ARRIVAL

Your former sergeant was an easy-going guy. If you arrived a few minutes late for work, he regarded it as "no big deal." Your newly appointed sergeant, however, is stringent about punctuality. Last week, you arrived 20 minutes late for your morning shift. The sergeant gave you an oral warning stating, "If it happens again, I'll write a disciplinary report." This morning, you find you have approximately 10 minutes to get to work. The drive usually takes 15 minutes. You consider driving your patrol car with the emergency lights on.

Ethically, what should you do?

_____

_____

_____

_____

_____

_____

_____

_____

_____

_____

_____

_____

_____

_____

Scenario 23

THE TIME LOG

All of the officers in your department are required to submit time logs for off-duty court appearances. Off-duty court appearances equate to time-and-a-half for pay purposes. It is virtually a common practice for the officers in your squad to give an inflated version of the length of time they spend in court. You are the reporting officer in an armed robbery case. After waiting 10 minutes for your case to be called, the clerk announces a continuance.

Ethically, how should you submit your log?

_____

_____

_____

_____

_____

_____

_____

_____

_____

_____

_____

_____

_____

_____

Scenario 24

THE PROSTITUTE

A well-known prostitute on your beat, Starlight, frantically waves you down as you start the midnight shift. Starlight tells you that her "client," a prominent attorney, beat her and kicked her in the ribs after their sexual encounter. In addition, she tells you he did not pay her for the services she rendered.

Ethically, what should you do?

_____

_____

_____

_____

_____

_____

_____

_____

_____

_____

_____

_____

_____

_____

_____

_____

Scenario 25

THE CLEANERS

Tomorrow, your cousin is getting married. On your way to work this morning, you bring your tuxedo to Quick Clean Laundry for dry cleaning and ironing. The laundry closes early today: 2 P.M. Your shift ends at 3 P.M. You consider stopping by the cleaners while on duty to pick up your tuxedo for the wedding.

Ethically, what should you do?

_____

_____

_____

_____

_____

_____

_____

_____

_____

_____

_____

_____

_____

_____

_____

Scenario 26

THE MOVIES

You are an off-duty corrections officer. You and your friend decide to see the horror movie playing at the local theater. You happen to be wearing a T-shirt with a badge imprinted on it. The cashier at the booth says, "Good evening, Officer. You and your friend can go in without charge."

Ethically, what should you do?

_____

_____

_____

_____

_____

_____

_____

_____

_____

_____

_____

_____

_____

_____

_____

Scenario 27

THE JOINT

You are a corrections officer in a medium-security facility. One of the inmates in your unit, Inmate Monroe, is eligible for parole in two weeks. You favorably regard Inmate Monroe as a model inmate and one who complies with the rules. During a cell search, you find a marijuana cigarette underneath Inmate Monroe's mattress.

Ethically, what should you do?

_____

_____

_____

_____

_____

_____

_____

_____

_____

_____

_____

_____

_____

_____

Scenario 52

The Domestic Dispute Call

While at the scene of a domestic dispute, your sergeant approaches you. He asks if one of your coworkers in an adjacent patrol area was at the scene earlier. The reason for the inquiry is that the officer failed to respond to an emergency call to which he had been dispatched. Apparently, the officer told the sergeant that he was delayed because he was assisting you with your call.

Ethically, what should you do?

_____

_____

_____

_____

_____

_____

_____

_____

_____

_____

_____

_____

_____

_____

_____

_____

_____

_____

Scenario 53

THE "GONE ON ARRIVAL" COMPLAINANT

You are flagged down by a citizen complaining that he had called the police several hours ago to report an armed robbery. He tells you that no one has responded to the call. When you check further, you discover that your friends and coworkers, riding as a two-person unit, were dispatched to the call earlier in the evening. Apparently, they checked back into service, advising that the complainant was "gone on arrival." This is not the only time this has occurred.

Ethically, what should you do?

_____

_____

_____

_____

_____

_____

_____

_____

_____

_____

_____

_____

_____

_____

Scenario 54

THE COCAINE

While you are investigating a homicide case as the lead investigator, the victim's wife tells you that she believes her husband was killed as a result of a large sum of money owed for several kilos of cocaine her husband received on consignment. She further states that the cocaine was "confiscated" by a patrol officer who stopped the victim and her for a traffic infraction but who just gave them a warning and left with the contraband.

Ethically, what should you do?

_____

_____

_____

_____

_____

_____

_____

_____

_____

_____

_____

_____

_____

_____

Scenario 55

THE VICE OFFICER

You are off duty and at home in your first-floor apartment. While there, you overhear a vice officer from your department warning another officer that a search warrant is going to be executed on the officer's father's residence and suggests that his father dispose of any paraphernalia that could be used as potential evidence.

Ethically, what should you do?

_____

_____

_____

_____

_____

_____

_____

_____

_____

_____

_____

_____

_____

_____

_____

_____

Scenario 56

The Nightclub Brawl

You are an off-duty officer helping a friend of yours who owns a nightclub. While working security at the entrance, a fight ensues between a well-known musician and an unruly patron. The musician punches the patron in the face. The patron is bleeding. You intervene and break up the fight. The musician takes you aside and says, "Here's $500. Let's forget this ever happened."

Ethically, what should you do?

_____

_____

_____

_____

_____

_____

_____

_____

_____

_____

_____

_____

_____

_____

_____

_____

Scenario 57

The Game

You are on patrol a few blocks from the baseball stadium where there is a championship game underway. You pull over a van with a broken tail light heading toward the stadium. When you approach the driver, you can tell that he is of Middle Eastern descent, as is the other man in the passenger seat. The driver appears calm, but the passenger seems a bit nervous. You ask them where they are headed and what they're up to. After stammering a bit, the driver finally says they are on their way to the game. Everything checks out, but you are very suspicious and are not comfortable letting them go.

   Ethically, what should you do?

_____

_____

_____

_____

_____

_____

_____

_____

_____

_____

_____

_____

_____

_____

_____

Scenario 58

THE SEAPORT

You are on patrol at the seaport, and you are sitting in your marked car next to the terminal. You notice that a certain car has passed your location a number of times. The passenger, who appears to be of Middle Eastern descent, is taking pictures of the terminal building. Otherwise, they are doing nothing wrong.

Ethically, what should you do?

_____

_____

_____

_____

_____

_____

_____

_____

_____

_____

_____

_____

_____

_____

_____

_____

Scenario 59

"High" School Kids

You are working a drug sting, and you notice a car of high school kids driving up to purchase some drugs. You immediately recognize one of the kids: a straight A student and quarterback of the high school football team; one of the best in the county. Also, his family is a well-known supporter of the police. The kid obviously has a tremendous future ahead of him, and you aren't 100% sure how to handle this. He is a passenger, and the driver appears to be the one buying the drugs. (Or, what if he was the one buying the drugs? Does it matter?)

Ethically, what should you do?

_____

_____

_____

_____

_____

_____

_____

_____

_____

_____

_____

_____

_____

Scenario 60

THE VISITING PARTNER

You are a newly hired officer and you are on patrol with your partner, a 10-year veteran. About three times a week, your partner visits his girlfriend at her home for about 30 to 40 minutes each visit, sometimes as much as an hour. He tells you to wait for him in the car and to get him only for an emergency. You know this is against the rules, and you are uncomfortable with this situation.

    Ethically, what should you do?

_____

_____

_____

_____

_____

_____

_____

_____

_____

_____

_____

_____

_____

_____

_____

_____

Scenario 61

The Whiskey

You are an officer on patrol with your partner. Almost every day, you notice that your partner takes a miniature bottle of whiskey out of his pocket and drinks from it. It is not enough to impair him, but just enough to relax him a bit, he tells you. He also tells you that he never consumes more than one of these per day, but you are not quite sure this is true. He takes some Listerine afterwards to get rid of the smell on his breath. You feel that he is a good cop and that the alcohol is not affecting his job in a negative way.

Ethically, what should you do?

_____

_____

_____

_____

_____

_____

_____

_____

_____

_____

_____

_____

_____

_____

Scenario 62

A Gay Matter

You and your partner are dispatched to an upscale neighborhood regarding a reported domestic dispute. Upon arrival, you meet Shane, a gay male, who is crying and tells you, "My lover, Ashton, was in bed with another guy, so I had to beat him up." Ashton has a bloody nose, a swollen right eye, and complains of abdominal pains. He shouts, "Arrest him, Officer!" Your partner says to you, "Come on dude, let's go and let these *ladies* work it out themselves."

Ethically, what should you do?

_____

_____

_____

_____

_____

_____

_____

_____

_____

_____

_____

_____

_____

_____

_____

Scenario 63

THE DRUNK JUDGE

You are a state highway patrol trooper on patrol. It is approximately 1:00 A.M. when you notice a black, new model Mercedes weaving in and out of traffic. You follow the vehicle, which comes to a stop at the side of the road. After pulling over the motorist, you approach the car. A Black gentleman stumbles out of his car. He has bloodshot eyes and with slurred speech starts screaming at you. He yells, "You stupid cop! How dare you pull me over? Don't you know who I am? I am Judge Mark Murphy of the District Court of Appeals! Don't even think of giving me a ticket, or I'll file a civil rights suit against you!"

Ethically, what should you do?

_____

_____

_____

_____

_____

_____

_____

_____

_____

_____

_____

_____

_____

_____

Scenario 64

THE SUBWAY SUSPECTS

You are an undercover plainclothes officer assigned to the subway station. It is 11:30 P.M. when three young males, who appear to be of Middle Eastern descent, board the subway. You decide to follow them. While on the subway, they engage in "rowdy" behavior—singing loudly, joking, and making the following comments to passengers, "Whaddya think we are going to do? Blow up the train? Boom!"

Ethically, what should you do?

_____

_____

_____

_____

_____

_____

_____

_____

_____

_____

_____

_____

_____

_____

_____

Scenario 65

THE ROCK STAR

You are an officer assigned to the airport in a large metropolitan city. You and your K-9 dog are charged with conducting sniff tests of packages or persons you deem suspicious. You are informed that a well-known rock star and his girlfriend are about to board flight 468. Proper procedure dictates that all passengers must walk through the screening device. When the rock star approaches, he walks around the screening device, not through it. You tell him, "Sir, I need you to walk through." He says, "Come on, man. Don't you know who I am? How about an autograph?" Meanwhile, the K-9 starts barking and you believe the rock star has drugs on him. You tell him you have to pat him down. In his shirt pocket, you find a white powder-like substance in a plastic Ziploc bag, which you believe is cocaine. Your dog starts going crazy after he sniffed it, confirming your belief that it is cocaine.

Ethically, what should you do?

_____

_____

_____

_____

_____

_____

_____

_____

_____

_____

_____

_____

_____

_____

_____

_____

_____

_____

_____

_____

_____

_____

_____

_____

_____

_____

_____

_____

_____

_____

_____

_____

_____

_____

_____

_____

_____

_____

Scenario 66

THE TRAINING RECORD

You are a sergeant assigned to the training bureau of your agency. Your state requires that all sworn officers must complete 40 hours of mandatory training every four years in order to maintain their certification. One morning, you are checking the records of officers from your department when Asst. Chief Robins enters your office and sits down. He says, "Listen, Sarge, I've got a problem. Only you can help me. I completed 24 hours of training and I need 16 more. I was scheduled to take a two-day Ethics course next week to satisfy the requirement, but I can't make it 'cause my kid's going out of town for a Little League game, and I promised him I'd be there. My certification will expire if I don't take this course. Do you think you can enter into the system that I took the course and passed? I'm scheduled to take the same course, but in three weeks, after my certification lapses, so can you just enter it now? It's no big deal. I could probably teach the class myself."

Ethically, what should you do?

_____

_____

_____

_____

_____

_____

_____

_____

_____

_____

_____

_____

Scenario 67

THE CHIEF'S DAUGHTER

It is approximately 2:10 A.M. when you receive a call from the dispatcher that a hit and run occurred one mile away from your location. The dispatcher describes the car as a red, newer model, 2-door BMW. The victim is an elderly man who has been airlifted to the hospital. The suspect is described as a young, blonde female, approximately 17 years old. You put on your lights and start driving southbound. Minutes later you spot the BMW swerving through traffic at a high rate of speed. You pursue the vehicle and stop the motorist. When you approach, the driver is crying. You recognize her; it is Brittney, the Chief's daughter. She says, "I think I killed someone. I'm so scared. Don't tell my dad."

Ethically, what should you do?

Scenario 68

The Dangerous Call

It is 3:20 A.M. and you get a call from the dispatcher of a robbery in progress. The location is one of the worst in the community, where drug use, prostitution, guns, and gangs rule the streets day and night. It is known that officers "take their time" responding to calls from this particular subdivision, because, quite frankly, it is a highly dangerous part of town. Several officers on your squad called in sick tonight, so you may not have a backup officer to assist you.

Ethically, what should you do?

_____

_____

_____

_____

_____

_____

_____

_____

_____

_____

_____

_____

_____

_____

Scenario 69

THE RACIST LIEUTENANT

You and your friend are newly promoted sergeants in a large suburban police department. You are African American; your friend is Mexican. This morning you both are scheduled to meet with Lieutenant Patrick McMurphy, a veteran supervisor of Irish descent, to talk about your new shifts and assignments. Lt. McMurphy congratulates both of you and says, "OK. Let's get down to business. You both have been assigned to midnights. You take the Black 'hood and you the Spanish 'hood. You should both feel right at home with your own kind, and enjoy your type of food. Good luck!"

Ethically, what should you do?

_____

_____

_____

_____

_____

_____

_____

_____

_____

_____

_____

_____

_____

_____

Scenario 70

The Executive Protection Detail

You are an African American sergeant who completed an intensive one-month executive protection training course. Your captain informs you that in a few days there is going to be a Ku Klux Klan conference and that the head of the Klan is the individual directly assigned to you to protect. You are outraged because you have knowledge that this particular individual hates Blacks, and philosophically, you do not agree with the practices of the Klan.

Ethically, what should you do?

_____

_____

_____

_____

_____

_____

_____

_____

_____

_____

_____

_____

_____

_____

_____

_____

Scenario 71

THE HOSTAGE STANDOFF

You are a member of a large, metropolitan SWAT team. At approximately Noon, your team is deployed to the local area high school where two white male teens are suspected of having taken approximately 60 students hostage in the school cafeteria. They are armed with shotguns. This morning, your teenage son complained of stomach pains, but you sent him to school anyway, the same school where this violent incident is occurring. The SWAT commander has not given the order yet to enter the premises. You are going crazy with anticipation (your son is in there), and you need to make sure he is OK.

   Ethically, what should you do?

_____

_____

_____

_____

_____

_____

_____

_____

_____

_____

_____

_____

_____

_____

Scenario 72

THE NARCOTICS SQUAD

You are a young detective who just received word that a plum assignment is coming your way. Since you started your career, you have always wanted to work in the undercover narcotics unit. The opportunity to do so is now one week away, as one of the members of the squad is retiring. To celebrate your new position, three of the guys from the narcotics division tell you they want to take you out to dinner and that they have a final "test" for you. After a pleasant dinner and conversation, your group leaves the restaurant and gets in the car. Detective Porter takes out a Ziploc bag containing a white, powder-like substance (which you believe is cocaine). He says, "OK. Here's the deal. If you're going to survive on the streets with those scumbags, you need to occasionally be able to use this crap, so they'll think you're one of them, and not one of us. So, go ahead, take a sniff and show us what you're made of."

Ethically, what should you do?

_____

_____

_____

_____

_____

_____

_____

_____

_____

_____

_____

_____

Scenario 73

The Ex's Daughter

You are a female corrections officer assigned to the Women's Detention Facility. Each evening you review the backgrounds of newly admitted inmates who will be under your supervision. After reviewing the files, you are surprised to see the name Virginia Scott, the daughter of your former boyfriend. You have not seen Virginia for years, and she has been sentenced for aggravated battery. You walk by her cell at approximately midnight. She is happy to see you and states that she is having anxiety attacks about being locked up and would like to go to the recreation room alone for a few minutes to relax and have a smoke. You know with certainty that nobody else is around, the other inmates are sleeping, and there won't be another officer on duty until 6:00 A.M.

Ethically, what should you do?

_____

_____

_____

_____

_____

_____

_____

_____

_____

_____

_____

_____

_____

_____

Scenario 74

YOUR SISTER'S BOYFRIEND

You are a veteran officer and have a close-knit relationship with your younger sister. Her new boyfriend, whom you've met, is a real loser. They have been dating for a few months, and she calls you several times a week to complain that he is verbally abusive to her and that she is certain he is dating other women. He is supposedly unemployed, yet she calls you to tell you that he just purchased a brand-new Porsche and is planning a trip to Colombia. She suspects he is trafficking cocaine and wants you to run a background on him through NCIC, which you know is prohibited for personal use, but you love her and despise him.

Ethically, what should you do?

_____

_____

_____

_____

_____

_____

_____

_____

_____

_____

_____

_____

_____

Scenario 75

10 Minutes

In 10 minutes, you will be off your patrol shift. You promised your son that you would see his football game tonight. (You promised several times before, and couldn't make it, due to last-minute calls.) As you drive back to the station, you observe a serious car accident involving three vehicles. It must have occurred seconds before you arrived, because the passengers and motorists are still in their cars. You know if you take this incident, you will be at the scene for at least an hour or two and miss your son's game (again). You also know that several officers are on vacation, so the squad is limited.

Ethically, what should you do?

_____

_____

_____

_____

_____

_____

_____

_____

_____

_____

_____

_____

_____

_____

_____

_____

5

Points to Ponder and Discuss

Respond in detail to each question. As you do, try to think about the struggles you may encounter.

1. What is your definition of an ethical officer?

   _____

   _____

   _____

2. What is your definition of an unethical officer?

   _____

   _____

   _____

3. Do you believe an officer who accepts a free cup of coffee or a discounted meal is acting appropriately or inappropriately? Does the cost matter?

   _____

   _____

   _____

4. If a "good" officer performs a "bad" act, does that make him or her ethical or unethical? Why?

_____

_____

_____

5. If a "bad" officer performs a "good" act, does that make him or her ethical or unethical? Why?

_____

_____

_____

6. Why did you decide to enter the criminal justice profession?

_____

_____

_____

7. Do you think the general public views officers as primarily ethical or unethical?

_____

_____

_____

8. Do you view the general public as primarily ethical or unethical?

_____

_____

_____

9. Is the public's perception of you as an officer important?

_____

_____

_____

10. Are most of your friends affiliated with the criminal justice field?

_____

_____

_____

11. Is it important for you to fit in with your fellow officers?

_____

_____

_____

12. Do you believe it is ever necessary for you to compromise your personal values in order to be part of the team?

_____

_____

_____

13. Do you believe that individuals in command positions at your department have achieved their status ethically or unethically?

_____

_____

_____

14. Do you believe that undercover investigations and operations are ethical or unethical?

_____

_____

_____

15. Do you feel a part of or apart from the community in which you work?

_____

_____

_____

16. Do you feel a part of or apart from the department for which you work?

_____

_____

_____

17. Do you feel a part of or apart from your family?

_____

_____

_____

18. Do you feel you have changed in any way(s) since becoming a recruit or officer?

_____

_____

_____

19. If you have changed, do you regard these changes as mainly positive or negative?

_____

_____

_____

20. To whom are you most loyal?

Yourself	_____	Your community	_____
Your family	_____	Your friends	_____
Your department	_____	Your religion	_____

21. Do you feel you are more likely to give in to or stand up to pressure from your colleagues?

_____

_____

_____

22. What pressures are you most likely to give in to?

Political   _____   Family   _____

Departmental   _____   Friends   _____

Media   _____   Other   _____

23. Would you follow a direct order from a supervisor if you believed the order was unethical or inappropriate?

   _____

   _____

   _____

24. Have you ever done something within the scope of your employment that you believe is unethical?

   _____

   _____

   _____

25. Are you able to separate your professional life from your personal life?

   _____

   _____

   _____

26. Should supervisors be held accountable for the unethical actions of their subordinates?

   _____

   _____

   _____

27. Do you think whistle blowers protect the public interest?

   _____

   _____

   _____

28. Do you think whistle blowers help or hurt the department?

   _____

   _____

   _____

29. As an officer, when is it OK to look the other way?

_____

_____

_____

30. As an officer, when is it OK to file a false report?

_____

_____

_____

31. As an officer, when is it OK to be aggressive?

_____

_____

_____

32. If a man steals a loaf of bread because he is starving, is his behavior ethical or unethical?

_____

_____

_____

33. If a juvenile steals a pack of cigarettes to impress his friends, is his behavior ethical or unethical?

_____

_____

_____

34. Does the act itself determine whether a behavior is ethical, or is it the individual's _intent_ that determines ethics?

_____

_____

_____

35. Are your official decisions ever influenced by another's race, age, gender, social status, or attitude?

_____

_____

_____

36. If you knew that a fellow officer participated in unethical conduct, what, if anything, would you do about it?

_____

_____

_____

37. Do you believe other officers are primarily ethical or unethical?

_____

_____

_____

38. If officers were paid higher salaries, do you think there would be fewer instances of unethical conduct?

_____

_____

_____

39. Is it ethical for departments to conduct routine drug tests of their employees?

_____

_____

_____

40. Do you believe that all officers must stick together regardless of the circumstances?

_____

_____

_____

41. What is your definition of *professionalism*?

   _____

   _____

   _____

42. What is your definition of *gratuity*?

   _____

   _____

   _____

43. What is your definition of *crossing the line*?

   _____

   _____

   _____

44. Do you believe an officer should adopt an *us vs. them* philosophy?

   _____

   _____

   _____

45. As an officer, do you believe that some laws are difficult to enforce?

   _____

   _____

   _____

46. What is the most unethical thing a police or corrections officer could do?

   _____

   _____

   _____

47. Would you have difficulty arresting someone you know (friend, neighbor, fellow officer, or family member)?

   _____

_____

_____

48. Why do you think some officers behave unethically and inappropriately?

_____

_____

_____

49. How do you view your present work environment? Is it generally supportive or nonsupportive?

_____

_____

_____

50. Do you believe one officer can make a difference?

_____

_____

_____

Final Question: Are you ethical even when no one is looking?

_____

_____

_____

6

Where Do We Go
from Here?

Are we able to rise above the O.J. Simpson case and the role Detective Mark Fuhrman played in it? Have we fully recovered from the graphic images of officers beating Rodney King while he was handcuffed on the pavement? It's difficult to say how citizens will perceive officers in the future if their memories remain focused on these disturbing isolated findings. If there is any way to gain citizens' trust of and respect for criminal justice personnel, it is through the continuous heroic actions taking place every day. The hundreds and thousands of men and women who so selflessly give of their time, their hearts, and their lives to make the streets safer for all of us should be *commended*. Although their stories of courage and sacrifice may not make headlines, we know that they represent the majority of police and corrections officers.

Early on in the workbook, we discussed six factors that influence an officer's decision to behave ethically and appropriately or unethically and inappropriately. Let's review those points.

First, an officer's *environment* refers to external influences: choices and behaviors of family members and peers as well as exposure to appropriate and inappropriate activities. An officer's *work environment* refers to how the officer perceives the role as well as those with whom he or she works.

Second, the *training academy* plays a part in how recruits interact with others and how instructors present the role of a criminal justice representative.

Third, the officer's *home life* refers to views parents may have instilled during his or her formative years as well as the support the officer presently receives from significant others.

Fourth, every officer has his or her *individual beliefs* about others and which behaviors they view as ethical or unethical for the profession.

Fifth, *citizens* affect an officer's decision-making ability by their conduct and demeanor toward the officer.

Sixth, *stress* must be managed effectively so the officer can be emotionally, physically, and intellectually fit for the rigorous duties he or she is called upon to perform.

At this time, we will address measures criminal justice administrators can take to encourage ethical conduct among police and corrections professionals.

Ways to Enforce Ethics

1. Identify in writing, within department policies and/or procedures, the specific behaviors that are inappropriate or unethical.
2. Identify in writing, within department policies and/or procedures, the specific consequences of inappropriate or unethical behaviors.
3. Implement ethics training seminars for all sworn and civilian personnel.
4. Conduct routine drug tests of all employees.
5. Reinforce positive behavior by rewarding ethical actions.
6. Encourage officers to report unethical behavior of fellow colleagues.
7. Hold employees and supervisors accountable for their actions and inactions.
8. Ask employees for their recommendations regarding ways to encourage an ethical workforce.
9. Create a working environment based on pride, praise, and professionalism.
10. Lead by example each and every day.

Also, professional police and corrections departments should have, in writing, a *value statement*. *A value statement represents the principles that officers and administrators regard as essential to the effective functioning of their department.* Following are two examples of value statements.

Police Value Statement

We, the officers of _____ Police Department, are committed to enforcing the laws, protecting the citizens, and preserving the peace. The following represents the values that we view as most important to our ethical and professional Police Department:

Value 1.   We will uphold the rights of all citizens regardless of race, color, creed, gender, culture, or religion.

Value 2.   We will conduct ourselves at all times with integrity, pride, and professionalism.

Value 3.   We will provide the best service possible to the citizens we have sworn to protect.

Value 4.   We will view crime prevention as the fundamental responsibility of our ethical and professional police department.

Value 5.   We will vigorously pursue those who commit criminal acts and those who threaten the safety and well-being of our citizens.

Create five more statements concerning police values:

Value 6.   We will _____

_____

_____

_____

Value 7.   We will _____

_____

_____

_____

Value 8.   We will _____

_____

_____

_____

Value 9.   We will _____

_____

_____

_____

Value 10.   We will _____

_____

_____

In order for the value statement to motivate representatives of a police department, roll call supervisors should ask a police officer, at least once a week, to read aloud the value statement at the close of a meeting.

Corrections Value Statement

We, the officers of _____ Corrections Department, are committed to ensuring the care, custody, and control of the offender population we serve. The following represents the values that we view as most important to our ethical and professional Corrections Department:

Value 1.   We will treat fairly all offenders regardless of race, color, creed, gender, culture, or religion.

Value 2.   We will conduct ourselves at all times with integrity, pride, and professionalism.

Value 3.   We will strive to work as a team in meeting the day-to-day challenges of our institution.

Value 4.   We will work cooperatively with public safety agencies to enhance the effectiveness of our department.

Value 5.   We will provide an environment that is safe and secure for offenders and staff.

Create five more statements concerning corrections values:

Value 6.   We will _____

_____

_____

_____

Value 7.   We will _____

_____

_____

_____

Value 8.   We will _____

_____

_____

_____

Value 9.   We will _____

_____

_____

_____

Value 10.   We will _____

_____

_____

_____

Again, to maximize the impact of the value statement, supervisors should ask a corrections officer, at least once a week, to read aloud the value statement at the close of a meeting.

What else can be done to encourage ethical choices and behaviors? Recruits and officers need to be mindful of the various situations they may encounter and what they should and should not do. We'll call this list, "Three Dos and a Don't."

Court

1. Do come prepared with the facts of a case.
2. Do respond politely to a defense attorney's questions.
3. Do tell the truth at all times.

Don't lose control during cross-examination.

Training Academy

1. Do interact with trainees, staff, instructors, and supervisors in a respectful manner.
2. Do learn all the lessons being taught to the best of your ability.
3. Do support your colleagues in their pursuit of success.

Don't violate Academy policies or procedures.

Gifts and Favoritism

1. Do decline offers of *free* anything.
2. Do treat individuals without favoritism or bias.
3. Do remember the code you promised to uphold.

Don't bend the rules; once something bends, it could become broken.

Citizens

1. Do provide the citizens of your community with your best service.
2. Do communicate courteously during vehicle stops and ticketing.

3. Do attend neighborhood crime watch meetings.

Don't lose your temper, even if a citizen loses his or her cool.

Private Life

1. Do think intelligently about how you conduct your private life.
2. Do choose friends who are law-abiding individuals.
3. Do communicate effectively about your feelings with significant others.

Don't do anything to shame your family or your department.

Facility

1. Do adopt a "firm but fair" philosophy with inmates.
2. Do cooperate with other officers and supervisors.
3. Do adhere to your department's rules and regulations.

Don't allow yourself to become manipulated by offenders.

Decision Making

1. Do think about what you were trained to do.
2. Do consider the consequences associated with unethical conduct.
3. Do follow through with what you took an oath to do.

Don't engage in any unfavorable conduct, on or off duty.

Finally, when you make a decision to behave a certain way, ask yourself this question:

"WOULD I FEEL COMFORTABLE HAVING MY BEHAVIOR TELEVISED ON THE LOCAL OR NATIONAL NEWS?"

You never know.

7

Answer Guide
to Scenarios

Note: It is the opinion of the author that the answers provided for the scenarios are consistent with ethical guidelines and policies in most states. If your responses differ, discuss why among your colleagues.

Scenario 1: The Club Sandwich

You should tell your fellow officers that you feel comfortable paying for your own lunch and that you plan to do so for the rest of your career!

Scenario 2: The Perjurer

Lying to protect another officer's mistake is a quick way to end an ethical career. Remember: One lie leads to many more. Telling the truth about an incident may be a bit of a stumble, but a stumble prevents a fall! Is the lie worth the fall? No!

Scenario 3: The False Report

Wrong! The kid does not have to pay for his actions when he has not committed a violation of the law. Creating facts to incriminate another is dishonest.

Scenario 4: **The Favor**

If you allow Inmate Jones to use the phone, you are rewarding his honesty. However, showing favoritism toward an inmate could lead to manipulation. Consult with your supervisor.

Scenario 5: **The Promotional Test**

You should study the material that you were told to study and decline your friend's offer of a sample copy of the test.

Scenario 6: **The Money**

As an individual in a supervisory position, you are called on to oversee the actions of other personnel. Therefore, you should question Sergeants Anderson and Foster about the money. Inform Internal Affairs about the matter if their answer does not explain the situation.

Scenario 7: **The Cheater**

You should have reported this incident right away. However, you are still obligated to file an anonymous complaint so that Officer Perez will be questioned by Internal Affairs.

Scenario 8: **The Wallet**

You should contact the owner and return the wallet, credit cards, identification, and cash (regardless of the amount)!

Scenario 9: **The Supervisor**

Have a meeting to advise them of what behaviors are acceptable and unacceptable. Then deal with each subsequent violation as it arises.

Scenario 10: **The Harasser**

When asked, attach an addendum to her report stating *specifically* what you heard Sergeant Richards say to her. Remember: Stand for something!

Scenario 11: **The Whistle Blower**

Most police and corrections officers fear being regarded as a "snitch" or "rat." However, failing to report a violation of law or policy when you have knowledge of a wrongful act could make you liable as well. You should inform your supervisor of the conversation you heard.

Scenario 12: The Truth

You should advise your nephew to tell the truth. Nothing can change the fact that your nephew used drugs as an adolescent. He should mention his involvement and start his career in law enforcement honestly!

Scenario 13: The Holiday Gift

You should thank Jerry for his appreciation of your service and decline the $100 bill.

Scenario 14: The Cadet

Favoritism is a form of unethical conduct. The cadet, whether a well-known politician's son or not, received three reprimands. He should be punished according to departmental policy.

Scenario 15: The Aggressor

Tell the captain what happened. You did nothing wrong; Officer Ward did.

Scenario 16: The Brother-in-Law

You have one option: Arrest him.

Scenario 17: The "Professional Courtesy" Approach

The concept of "professional courtesy" is debatable. Does it mean you will overlook *all* inappropriate practices of a fellow officer? Will you overlook *some* things and not others? Is this favoritism? If so, the *code of ethics* states, "Enforce the law without favor." If you have used your discretion and allowed other speeders to go with only a warning, you are treating him without favor.

Scenario 18: The Dinner Break

You are a public servant. You should help the woman retrieve her keys from the vehicle before you finish your meal, unless department policy prohibits you from assisting in this situation. Some departments have adopted such a policy because these calls keep them from their law enforcement duties.

Scenario 19: **The Crank Call**

It does not matter how many crank calls have come in. It is an officer's responsibility to investigate a shooting-related call. Investigate!

Scenario 20: **The Skimmer**

Officer Burton's behavior is not justifiable! He's stealing; therefore, the appropriate disciplinary action must be taken.

Scenario 21: **The Freebie**

You should thank the new owner of the convenience store for his appreciation of your service. Respectfully decline his offer of free items. Continue to pay for your gum, soda, and potato chips.

Scenario 22: **The Late Arrival**

Misusing your patrol vehicle by using the emergency lights in a non-emergency situation is neither prudent nor appropriate and may expose you to civil liability should the misuse result in an accident.

Scenario 23: **The Time Log**

Although some officers submit inflated versions of the time they spend in court, the ethical officer should submit a time log that accurately reflects the actual time he or she spends in court. Check your department policy.

Scenario 24: **The Prostitute**

The victim in this scenario may appear to lack credibility because she is a prostitute. However, she alleges she incurred a beating, and you should gather the facts and write an incident report. If you have other evidence, you should also arrest her for prostitution because she just admitted the crime to you.

Scenario 25: **The Cleaners**

Check your department policy regarding this matter. Typically, you should pick up your tuxedo on your personal time; you should not pick up your tuxedo while on duty.

Scenario 26: **The Movies**

You should thank the cashier for the offer of free movie tickets and tell him or her that you will pay for your own movie ticket.

Scenario 27: The Joint

As a corrections officer, you are responsible for ensuring the care, custody, and control of inmates. You are not called on to overlook violations of facility policy. Therefore, because you found a marijuana cigarette during a cell search, you should confiscate the contraband, question Inmate Monroe, and write a report.

Scenario 28: The Interrogation

Check state and federal statutes regarding lawful procedures for the questioning of defendants.

Scenario 29: The Race Card

Race is irrelevant. In this case, you have enough probable cause to arrest both juveniles, and you should arrest them for the crime you believe they have committed.

Scenario 30: The Use of Force Report

All officers know excessive force is unethical and inappropriate. You witnessed Officer Nelson using excessive force on Inmate Hagerty; therefore, you should inform the unit supervisor of the incident.

Scenario 31: The Defense Attorney

When officers testify in court, they *swear* to tell the truth. You should respond honestly to the defense attorney's question. After this experience, you will never again forget to read Miranda warnings to a subject!

Scenario 32: The Old Man

Abe Lawrence committed a crime: petty theft. The manager wants him arrested, and Mr. Lawrence admits to stealing the items; therefore, you should arrest him.

Scenario 33: The "Pissed-Off" Officer

This scenario represents a turning point in a rookie officer's career. A senior officer asks you to write a false report, based on a false charge, which led to a false arrest. He made the arrest, so he should file the report, not you. Inform your supervisor of the incident.

Scenario 34: The Boozer

What are you going to do about it? You observe a fellow officer, while he is on duty, in an intoxicated state. You should notify your supervisor *immediately* before the officer or someone else gets hurt.

Scenario 35: The Sleeper

First, question Officer Adams to confirm if he was sleeping. If so, you should inform the shift commander of the incident.

Scenario 36: The "Nose Candy"

If the incident occurs within your jurisdiction, make an arrest! If it is outside your jurisdiction, notify local authorities. This is a felony! You are required to take action.

Scenario 37: The Aggressive Partner

You should intervene and stop your partner from abusing the juvenile. In addition, you should notify your supervisor of the incident.

Scenario 38: The Parking Ticket

You should explain to Dave that a vehicle without a disability decal parked in a handicapped zone warrants a ticket. Pay for your own lunch.

Scenario 39: The Liquor

You should thank Mr. Newfeld for offering you a bottle of liquor and respectfully decline his gift.

Scenario 40: The Brunette

As discussed earlier, ethics in the home is as important as ethics in the workplace; therefore, tell your wife where you've been. (If she gets mad at you, don't go out with the secretary again.)

Scenario 41: The Tune-Up

You should tell Mike to prepare another bill because you will pay for the service provided.

Scenario 42: The "Friendly" Officer

You should tell Officer Daniels that his behavior is unacceptable and inappropriate. Write a report about the incident and seek the appropriate disciplinary action.

Scenario 43: The Stolen Property

You should inform the supervisor about the incident and write a report.

Scenario 44: The Instigator

You should tell the shift commander what Officer Garcia said, which you believe instigated the confrontation.

Scenario 45: The Tutor

You should encourage Rudy to put forth his best effort. You can offer him guidance and support; however, you should not take the exam for him.

Scenario 46: The Wife Beater

You have enough probable cause to make an arrest, and that's what you should do. Arrest him.

Scenario 47: The Celebrity Inmate

Celebrity or not, you are supposed to treat inmates fairly and without favoritism. Let him know that's what you're planning to do. Decline his offer of baseball tickets.

Scenario 48: The Cuddly Cops

Inform your immediate supervisor about the officers' unethical behavior.

Scenario 49: The Fraternity Brother

Although fraternity brothers pledge their loyalty to one another, you have pledged your loyalty to the citizens, to your department, and to the state! Arrest him.

Scenario 50: The Jokers

This is not a joke! This is sexual harassment, and it must not be tolerated anytime or anywhere! Tell the sergeant what you know.

Scenario 51: **The Prostitute's Bracelet**

Contact your sergeant immediately and inform him or her of the situation.

Scenario 52: **The Domestic Dispute Call**

Be honest and tell the sergeant that you never observed the officer at the scene of the call.

Scenario 53: **The "Gone on Arrival" Complainant**

Handle the call and notify your supervisor to talk to the complainant.

Scenario 54: **The Cocaine**

This is a highly sensitive issue. Contact Internal Affairs with the information, and refer the victim's wife to an Internal Affairs investigator. Proceed with your investigation.

Scenario 55: **The Vice Officer**

Again, this is a highly sensitive issue. Internal Affairs should be contacted with the pertinent information.

Scenario 56: **The Nightclub Brawl**

Decline his $500 offer and arrest him for aggravated battery.

Scenario 57: **The Game**

Do you have reasonable suspicion? Probable cause? If so, check the tag and give yourself peace of mind.

Scenario 58: **The Seaport**

You should stop the vehicle. Ask the driver and passenger why they are at the seaport. Do they work there? Are they taking a cruise? If no, they need to leave.

Scenario 59: **"High" School Kids**

You need to stop the vehicle, question passengers and motorist, and make arrests (even of the straight-A student) if warranted.

Scenario 60: The Visiting Partner

You need to inform your sergeant of the matter. This violates policy, and you could be in trouble if you stay quiet about it.

Scenario 61: The Whiskey

You should inform your supervisor that you believe your partner may have a drinking problem. Many feel they are doing their friends/colleagues a favor by keeping quiet, but a friend helps a friend who needs help.

Scenario 62: A Gay Matter

You should treat this domestic issue in a similar manner to a male/female relationship. There is just cause to make an arrest, and this couple should not be treated differently because they are homosexual.

Scenario 63: The Drunk Judge

You should conduct a field sobriety test, and issue a ticket for reckless driving. Depending upon the results of the Breathalyzer test, you may have cause for an arrest. Also, in your report, document verbatim, in quotes, what he said to you.

Scenario 64: The Subway Suspects

You can check their IDs.

Scenario 65: The Rock Star

Arrest him!

Scenario 66: The Training Record

Don't do it! You must respectfully decline as your job and certification (as well as his) would be ruined.

Scenario 67: The Chief's Daughter

Contact your supervisor immediately. This is a serious crime involving a familiar party. It simply cannot be dismissed.

Scenario 68: **The Dangerous Call**

Take the call, but request backup immediately.

Scenario 69: **The Racist Lieutenant**

Both of you need to inform Internal Affairs of the meeting as well of Lt. McMurphy's statements.

Scenario 70: **The Executive Protection Detail**

In this case, you must put personal feelings aside and perform your duty to protect this individual.

Scenario 71: **The Hostage Standoff**

Do not take matters into your own hands. This could get you or others killed. Wait for the SWAT commander to give the order to enter the building.

Scenario 72: **The Narcotics Squad**

Are you kidding? Don't even think for a second about sniffing anything.

Scenario 73: **The Ex's Daughter**

Do not grant Virginia special permission. Treat her as you would every other inmate.

Scenario 74: **Your Sister's Boyfriend**

Tell your sister to dump this guy and don't run a background check through NCIC.

Scenario 75: **10 Minutes**

You need to take this call and handle the incident. Make it up to your son by planning a special weekend activity when you can schedule time off from work.

A

Law Enforcement Code of Ethics

As a Law Enforcement Officer, my fundamental duty is to serve mankind; to safeguard lives and property; to protect the innocent against deception, the weak against oppression or intimidation, and the peaceful against violence or disorder; and to respect the Constitutional rights of all people to liberty, equality, and justice.

I will keep my private life unsullied as an example to all; maintain courageous calm in the face of danger, scorn, or ridicule; develop self-restraint; and be constantly mindful of the welfare of others. Honest in thought and deed in both my personal and official life, I will be exemplary in obeying the laws of the land and the regulations of my department. Whatever I see or hear of a confidential nature or that is confided to me in my official capacity will be kept ever secret, unless revelation is necessary in the performance of my duty.

I will never act officiously or permit personal feelings, prejudices, animosities, or friendships to influence my decisions. With no compromise for crime and with relentless prosecution of criminals, I will enforce the law courteously and appropriately without fear or favor, malice or ill will, never employing unnecessary force or violence and never accepting gratuities.

I recognize the badge of my office as a symbol of public faith, and I accept it as a public trust to be held so long as I am true to the ethics of the police service. I will constantly strive to achieve these objectives and ideals, dedicating myself before God to my chosen profession . . . law enforcement.

(Reprinted with permission from the International Association of Chiefs of Police.)

B

American Correctional Association Code of Ethics

Preamble

The American Correctional Association expects of its members unfailing honesty, respect for the dignity and individuality of human beings, and commitment to professional and compassionate service. To this end, we subscribe to the following principles:

1. Members shall respect and protect the civil and legal rights of all individuals.
2. Members shall treat every professional situation with concern for the welfare of the individuals involved and with no intent of personal gain.
3. Members shall maintain relationships with colleagues to promote mutual respect within the profession and improve the quality of service.
4. Members shall make public criticisms of their colleagues or their agencies only when warranted, verifiable, and constructive.
5. Members shall respect the importance of all disciplines within the criminal justice system and work to improve cooperation with each segment.
6. Members shall honor the public's right to information and share information with the public to the extent permitted by law, subject to individuals' right to privacy.
7. Members shall respect and protect the right of the public to be safeguarded from criminal activity.
8. Members shall refrain from using their positions to secure personal privileges or advantages.

211

9. Members shall refrain from allowing personal interest to impair objectivity in the performance of duties while acting in an official capacity.

10. Members shall refrain from entering into any formal or informal activity or agreement that presents a conflict of interest or that is inconsistent with the conscientious performance of duties.

11. Members shall refrain from accepting any gift, service, or favor that is or appears to be improper or that implies an obligation inconsistent with the free and objective exercise of professional duties.

12. Members shall clearly differentiate between personal views/statements/positions and views/statements/positions made on behalf of the agency or the Association.

13. Members shall report to appropriate authorities any corrupt or unethical behavior for which there is sufficient evidence to justify review.

14. Members shall refrain from discriminating against any individual because of race, gender, creed, national origin, religious affiliation, age, or any other type of prohibited discrimination.

15. Members shall preserve the integrity of private information, members shall refrain from seeking information on individuals beyond that which is necessary to implement their responsibilities and perform their duties, and members shall refrain from revealing nonpublic data unless expressly authorized to do so.

16. Members shall make appointments, promotions, and dismissals in accordance with established civil service rules, applicable contract agreements, and individual merit rather than furtherance of personal interests.

17. Members shall respect, promote, and contribute to a workplace that is safe, healthy, and free of harassment in any form.

Adopted August 1975 at the 105th Congress of Correction.
Revised August 1990 at the 120th Congress of Correction.
Revised August 1994 at the 124th Congress of Correction.

Bibliography

The following resources are recommended for further reading.

Bennett, Wayne, and Hess, Karen. *Management and Supervision in Law Enforcement*. California: Wadsworth Publishing Co., 2001.

Close, Daryl, and Meier, Nicholas. *Morality in Criminal Justice: An Introduction to Ethics*. California: Wadsworth Publishing Co., 1995.

Elliston, Frederick, and Feldberg, Michael. *Moral Issues in Police Work*. New Jersey: Rowan and Allanheid, 1985.

Facione, Peter; Scherer, Donald; and Attig, Thomas. *Ethics and Society* (Second Edition). New Jersey: Prentice Hall, 1991.

Florida Department of Law Enforcement. *Basic Recruit Training Program for Police and Corrections*. 1993.

Fried, Charles. *Right and Wrong*. Massachusetts: Howard University Press, 1978.

Goldstein, Herman. *Police Corruption*. District of Columbia, Washington, DC: Police Foundation, 1975.

Hansen, Paul. *Creative Stress Management for Law Enforcement and Corrections*. Colorado: Creative Stress Management, Ltd., 1981.

Mappes, Thomas, and Zembaty, Jane. *Social Ethics: Morality and Social Policy*. New York: McGraw-Hill, Inc., 1977.

Pollock, Joycelyn. *Ethics in Crime and Justice: Dilemmas and Decisions* (Second Edition). California: Wadsworth Publishing Co., 1994.

Ruchelman, Leonard. *Who Rules the Police?* New York: New York University Press, 1973.

Stinchcomb, Jeanne. *Managing Stress: Performing Under Pressure*. Maryland: American Correctional Association, 1995.